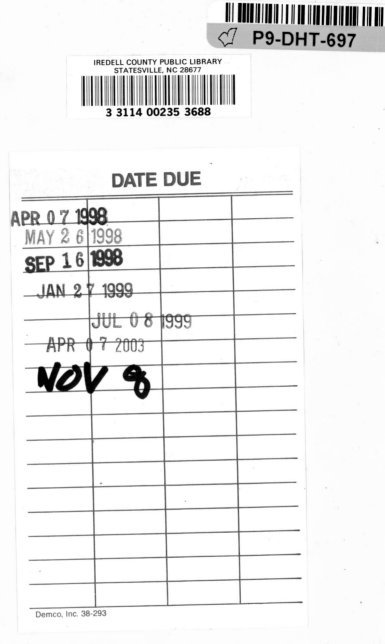

DATE DUE

APR 0 7 1998		
MAY 2 6 1998		
SEP 1 6 1998		
JAN 2 7 1999		
JUL 0 8 1999		
APR 0 7 2003		
NOV 8		

Demco, Inc. 38-293

Wasted

TALES OF A GENX DRUNK

Wasted

Mark Gauvreau Judge

HAZELDEN®

Hazelden
Center City, Minnesota 55012-0176
1-800-328-0094
1-612-257-1331 (24-hour FAX)
http://www.hazelden.org
(World Wide Web site on Internet)

Library of Congress Cataloging-in-Publication Data
Judge, Mark Gauvreau, 1964-
    Wasted : tales of a GenX drunk / Mark Gauvreau Judge.
        p.   cm.
    Includes bibliographical references.
    ISBN 1-56838-142-5
    1. Alcoholism–United States. 2. Alcoholics–Rehabilitation–United States.
3. Generation X–United States. I. Title
HV5229.J83   1997
362.292'8'092–dc21
[B]   97-9225
                                                                                  CIP
            02 01 00 99 98 97   9 8 7 6 5 4 3 2 1

Book design by Civic Design of Northeast Minneapolis
Typesetting by Universal Press

Editor's note

Hazelden offers a variety of information on chemical dependency and related areas. Our publications do not necessarily represent Hazelden's programs, nor do they officially speak for any Twelve Step organization.

This book is based on actual experiences. In some cases, the names and details have been changed to protect the privacy of the people involved.

The following publishers have generously given permission to use material from copyrighted works: From *The Thirsty Muse.* Copyright © 1989 by Thomas A. Dardis. Reprinted by permission of Ticknor & Fields/Houghton Mifflin Company. All rights reserved. From *Under the Influence.* Copyright © 1984 by James R. Milam and Katherine Ketcham. Reprinted by permission of Bantam, a division of Bantam, Doubleday, Dell Publishing Group, Inc.

*To my parents
and Alice Mitchell Hurley*

a c k n o w l e d g m e n t s

The people without whom this book would not have been written and life would be a bore. First, my family—my brothers Joe and Mike, my sister Alyson, sister-in-law Marianne, brother-in-law Marty, nieces Mary and Kathleen, and aunt Anita. Also the wonderful cousins: the McDonoughs, MacKalls, Mitchells, and Hurleys. Special appreciation to Joe Hurley, whose love, support, and humor have often brought me from despair to laughter.

My agent, Deborah Grosvenor, whose persistence, criticism, and encouragement were invaluable to finishing this project.

William Barrett Haynos, the best friend anyone could wish for and the best doctor in Washington.

Caryn Pernu and Dan Odegard at Hazelden. Julian Mazor and Charles McCarry, two brilliant writers whose wisdom, encouragement, and advice gave me courage to stick with it.

Almost last and certainly not least: Steve Ochs, Greg Hartley, and the faculty past and present at Prep, Monsignors Ranieri and Enzler, the kids from Country Place, Jim Thompson, Jason Rubis, Frankie Manning, Alex Jasperson, Ella Fitzgerald, Christopher Lasch, Jesus, Thomas Merton, Jack Kirby.

And finally, the Prep boys, who continue to be a constant reminder that life is supposed to be fun.

chapter

A Potential Alcoholic

"GO MAN, GO!" RONNIE SHOUTED. "YOU GOT IT! YOU'RE SWINGIN'!"

The bartender didn't know how to dance very well so I gave her a strong lead, twirling her under my arm and pulling her back to my side. I lowered her into a dip right as the song—"One O'clock Jump" by Count Basie—came to a close.

"Man, that was amazing!" Shane, my best friend, said as I sat back down at our table. "That deserves a shot." He waved for the waiter.

"No," I said, catching his arm. "I'm off the sauce."

He looked confused and lowered his arm. "You're not becoming a recovery junkie on me, are you?"

"Let's just say that I'm not having any today," I said, glancing at Ronnie. He smiled and winked at me.

"Wonderful," Shane said. "Next thing you know you'll be telling me about how your dysfunctional childhood turned you into a drunk."

"Dysfunctional childhood doesn't cause alcoholism," I said. "Biology does."

After ten years of drinking and a lifetime of misinformation about alcohol, I was ready to face the truth of my addiction. And the truth was that while my childhood and community may have increased my exposure to the drug alcohol, a genetic disposition to alcoholism was what had triggered my addiction.

My childhood, in fact, had been fairly normal. I was raised in Potomac, Maryland, a small town about twenty miles outside of Washington, DC. My father worked in Washington for the Labor Department under President Eisenhower, but being a nature lover, he wanted to live in the country. In the late fifties, when my family moved there, Potomac was mostly hills, horses, and trees.

The son of Joe Judge, a famous first-baseman for the Washington Senators, my father, also named Joe, was the antithesis of the typical jock. Quiet, fiercely intellectual, highly educated and artistic, he had excelled aesthetically and academically where his father had athletically.

My mother, Phyllis, was a pretty Irish-Catholic brunette from Massachusetts. She had lost her own mother to cancer when she was sixteen and had grown up with a hard-drinking father. The oldest of three, she had worked to support her family since she was a teenager. She had been a telephone operator, a teacher, and a nurse in the Korean war, and was teaching in Washington when she met my father in a bar in Chevy Chase.

After getting married, she and my father shunned the city in favor of the small town of Potomac. There they had four kids— Joe, Michael, Alyson, and, in 1964, me. All of us were two years apart. We lived in a pseudo-colonial house surrounded by dirt roads, trees, and very few other houses. Indeed, we were so isolated that when my sister was a toddler, she accidentally got out of the house during a snowstorm, crawled across the street, and appeared, unharmed, at our neighbor's front porch. There were no streetlights, and we could let our dog, Christopher Robin, out unleashed and unfenced for hours—even days—at a time.

For most of my adolescence, Potomac was a small town rather than the sprawling, anonymous, congested suburb it has since become. Our few neighbors and the collection of stores a few miles away in "the village" were like characters out of mythic small-town America. George, the local owner of the District General Store, was a bald, skinny old man who personified the rural atmosphere of old Potomac. He delivered groceries to my mother when she was pregnant, and had a sense of humor full of biting sarcasm. One of my mother's favorite stories about George was the time a wealthy woman who had just moved to Potomac came into the DGS with a friend and claimed to be appalled at the high price of lettuce. "Ninety-nine cents for a head of lettuce," she sniveled to her friend. "The owner can take that and shove it up his ass."

As it happened, George was just a few feet away, pricing some fruit. "I'd love to lady," he rejoined, "but I've already got a 79-cent cucumber up there."

Because it was the country, my mother let us roam free. My earliest memories are of feeling overwhelmed in the presence of nature. One of my most vivid memories is of walking down Rock

Run on Halloween, clutching the hands of my older brother Michael and older sister Alyson on either side of me and feeling almost paralyzed with fear and excitement at the complete darkness surrounding us. This was before electric pollution drove the night from Potomac, and you could take a walk and feel the powerful magic of the night.

As more and more people moved into Potomac, that magic became more elusive. Potomac lost any sense of place, identity, and local color. Suburban sprawl of postwar America has had a disastrous effect on the civic life of America, and Potomac is a prime example. Where once there was a little league field that doubled as a fairground there is now a shopping center, although one without corner shops, bars, a main street, or any other spaces of civic and communal life. It became just like every other suburb in America: a bunch of unconnected houses with people who never see each other and need their cars to get a pint of milk.

Indeed, because of the growing blandness of Potomac, Washington had a special appeal to me as a child. Although DC wasn't much more than a southern town at the time, I always felt a breathless excitement when my father would take us downtown. By the time I was born, he had left the Labor Department and had moved on to a job in journalism with the *National Geographic,* whose offices are just a couple blocks from the White House. Our visits to him gave me a small taste of urban life. In neighborhoods like Chevy Chase, Cleveland Park, and Georgetown there was activity, street life, and stores you could walk to. From the time I was young, I knew that it was how I wanted to live.

Still, for a child, Potomac in the 1960s could be a wonderful place. Our house was surrounded by trees and farms, and my brothers and sister were allowed to explore the countryside uninhibited. We all got along, and aside from the occasional skinned knee, most of life was pleasant.

There was, however, a dark undercurrent to the rustic tranquillity: alcohol. My father was a daily drinker. Every evening he would arrive home in his black Volkswagen Beetle and my mother would fix him a drink, usually a martini or vodka tonic, and he would spend the rest of the evening drinking. Some of my earliest memories are from Halloween, when my father would take us trick-or-treating. He always wore a devil costume and carried a large glass filled with a vodka tonic, and whenever it was empty, he would offer it to the neighbor behind the door and sing the Doors song "Come on Baby, Light My Fire."

The neighbor would laugh and give him a refill. Early on I equated alcohol with laugher and good times, as well as intellectual integrity. My father was a brilliant man whose job at "the Geo," as we called it, was to travel the world and write about it. When he wasn't drinking and writing on the other side of the world, he drank at home. He would spend hours in his den, reading, writing poetry, or going over ancient maps, always with a drink by his side. When he drank he would sometimes become thoughtful, funny, and reflective, discussing everything from the nature of the conflict in the Middle East to his belief in UFOs. I wanted to be like him, maybe even become a famous writer, and I knew that famous writers—Faulkner, Hemingway, Fitzgerald—drank.

My father, like these writers, could also be unpredictable. While booze could make my father funny, it also made him brooding, untouchable, apathetic, and mean. In 1974, when I was about ten, I had a crush on a neighbor girl, a secret that was exposed by one of my friends at a Fourth of July party. I was so mortified that I hid in my room and cried. My father heard me and came in to investigate. But he had been drinking and offered no solace. He sat there with his drink in one hand and watched me weep, as if he was a zoologist studying chimpanzees. Then he called in Joe and Mike and they all sat there waiting to figure out what was wrong. When I finally revealed my shame, my father acted surprised. *This hysterical display was about a girl?* He had thought that something was really wrong. He then got up in disgust and went back to the party, followed by Mike. "Don't worry about it," my brother Joe said. "He's just drunk." Joe is one of the most gentle and kind people I've ever met, and at times like that he often became the parental figure.

However, at such times I also went to my mother for comfort. After her mother's death at a young age, my mother had raised her brother and sister, and she had powerful maternal instincts that could make any problem go away. Once when I was a child, I was suffering from a splitting earache, and they tried everything to try to get the pain to stop—drops, pills, everything. Finally my mother took me on her lap and started to read to me, and the pain vanished. Incredibly, whenever she would stop reading, the pain would flare again.

While I grew up used to my father drinking heavily, I didn't get an indication that he was any worse than anyone else until he went streaking. It was late after a dinner party and my parents were both drunk when the topic of streaking, which was big in the mid-1970s, came up. One of the neighbors, an austere conservative, launched into a windy tirade about the moral decline of American culture and how there was no more salient example of our ethical slide than streaking. My father, an Irish-Catholic Democrat with a strong moral center, was never more outraged than when confronted with what he saw as false piety. Like his father, Dad was not a yeller or screamer; he took his revenge through sarcasm and humor.

In this case, his best response was to strip down to a pair of army boots and go for a jog around the neighborhood. Although our neighborhood was still pretty desolate, one woman who lived down the street did report a sighting. Apparently, she had been in her kitchen and had glanced out her front door to see a flash of white.

While everyone else in the family and many of the neighbors thought that the streaking was hysterical, and my father became something of a folk hero, I was deeply humiliated by the episode. I had a perception that all the other families in Potomac were perfect units with two loving parents, including fathers who didn't drink and who taught their sons how to ride a bike and throw a curve ball. My father was always too tired to do any of these things, but he did have enough energy to get drunk and run naked down the street.

Yet, despite his frequent emotional coldness, my father could occasionally be loving. The way he showed this was through literature and learning. In the pitch darkness of Potomac, he would bring us into the backyard and name the constellations as we peeked through his telescope. His den had wall-to-wall books, and he would spend hours showing us old poems or children's books from his own childhood in the 1930s.

He was also fiercely protective of us. When I was eleven he was assigned to do a story on Florida, and as part of it he got to take the entire family to Disney World. We went in August, and on the train ride down I was so excited I could barely sleep.

However, even in Disney World, with its romping cartoon

charters and ersatz American mythos, the dark underside of life lurked. The photographer assigned to shoot my father's story was a man named Clay Price. He was young and, like many *Geographic* photographers, considered himself something of a playboy. He had his girlfriend Vicki with him on the trip, and I immediately fell in love with him. With his flashy smile, casual, happy-go-lucky style and cameras swinging from his neck, he seemed like the antithesis of my father.

One afternoon Clay and Vicki took me and my sister Alyson, who was thirteen, out for ice cream. On the way home we were driving by the ocean when Clay suddenly pulled the car over.

"You guys want to go swimming?" he asked.

"Yeah!" we shouted back.

At first, I thought he was kidding. We didn't have bathing suits on, and my parents would never dream of doing anything this spontaneous.

"Let's go!" he called, clapping his hands.

We scrambled out of the car. We had stopped on a remote part of the highway and the beach was empty. It was late in the day and the tide was coming in, and the surf looked kind of rough. I hadn't learned how to swim yet, but wanted to go anyway. I could stick close to the shore.

We raced down to the water. Before I knew what was happening, Clay had swept me up in his arms and was dragging me out to sea. I began to panic, clutching at clumps of hair on his chest.

"I don't know how to swim," I shouted at him over the waves.

"I gotcha," he said, taking me out further.

We stayed out for about an hour, Vicki and Alyson swimming closer to the shore. Finally as the sun was going down, we trundled back to the car, soaked and exhausted.

"Wait a minute," Clay said. "If we sit in the car like this it'll ruin the seats." He dug into his trunk and found three towels. He gave one to Vicki, one to Alyson, and kept one for himself.

"You're the smallest, and I know how we can dry your clothes. Take them off."

I just looked at him. Was he kidding?

"Come on," he said with a smile, "take 'em off."

I complied. I had grown up with five authority figures in the house and would often just reply to a direct command.

I slipped off my shorts and T-shirt, then retreated into the backseat. Clay took my clothes and hung them on the antenna.

We sped away, my clothes flapping like a flag in a monsoon. I started to cry.

"Give him his clothes back!" my sister yelled, her voice thin in the winds whipping through the car.

"Sorry," Clay said. "They're drying."

My sister leaned over. "It's okay," she said. "I'm telling Dad when we get back."

I crouched lower and lower in the backseat, mortified. We were almost back to the hotel when Clay decided to pull into the drive-through of a fast-food place. I was now in the well of the backseat, covering my crotch so no one in the restaurant could see me from the window.

When we got back to the hotel, I was almost in tears. I went to my room and put on some dry clothes. Then I told my father what had happened.

He went nuts. Or at least, what passed in him for going nuts. He told me to wait in my room. Then about a half hour later, he came by to get me and brought me down to their room. Sitting there were my mother, Clay, and Vicki. Clay looked as though he had just seen a ghost. He didn't acknowledge me or move a muscle.

I took a few steps into the room, then my father held up his hand and I stopped.

"Mark," he said. "I want you to tell me exactly what happened today on the beach. Take your time."

Slowly, I recounted the story again.

"Okay," my dad said. "You can go. Mike and Joe are waiting for you in their room. You guys can order room service."

I left. It wasn't until I was older that I heard what had happened after I had left. My father had told Clay that he was lucky he didn't beat him to within an inch of his life right there, and that they would never work together again. My father said that if he ever heard of Clay pulling another stunt like that with anyone else, he would make sure he was fired.

Luckily for Clay, the rest of the vacation went smoothly. The highlight was when we got to take part in a parade through Disney World. We rode on a fire truck with Mickey, Goofy, and Snow White—who gave me a T-shirt then kissed me, much to my embarrassment—and Clay took pictures of the whole thing. The only one who seemed miserable was my oldest brother, Joe, who was eighteen. He had a low threshold for phoniness, and to him Disney World was about as unhip as you could get.

But while Joe mostly kept his cynicism to himself and stayed out of trouble, I seemed to have come into the world looking for trouble. Doctors have called it attention-deficit disorder, psychiatrists have cited my behavior as a cry for attention from my distant, drinking father, but at the end of the day I simply had a problem with authority.

It began early. When I was an infant, my family went on a trip to Rehoboth Beach on the Eastern Shore, a resort three hours from Washington. On the drive down, I sat on my mother's lap in the front seat. It was the middle of the summer, and since our station wagon didn't have air-conditioning, we had the windows rolled down. My mother had brought three bottles to keep me quiet, and when I started to fidget in her lap she gave me one. I sucked on it for a few seconds, then promptly tossed it out the window.

She gave me another. I sucked on it for a few seconds, then hurled it out also.

My brothers and sister started to laugh from the backseat.

"You're down to one bottle," my mother said, laughing. "You better make the most of this one."

She gave me the last bottle. Out the window it went.

Needless to say, I was dry for the rest of the trip.

A few years later, I was with my mother at the store when I saw something I wanted. She said no, and I threw a tantrum. I was so mad that on the way home I refused to ride up front with her and sat in the backseat with the groceries. I was sulking when I noticed a football-sized object sticking out of one of the bags. I peered closer: it was a Virginia baked ham. Slowly, I lifted the ham out of the bag and raised it over my mother's head.

She never knew what hit her. The blow to the back of her head almost made her drive off the side of the road. She jolted to a stop and yanked me over the seat, turning me on my stomach and spanking me until she couldn't lift her arm.

By coincidence, a police officer had been driving behind us. He had seen the whole thing. He pulled up beside my mother, slowed to a stop, and began applauding.

Despite such episodes, my parents weren't overly concerned

about my behavior. In the early seventies they enrolled me at Our Lady of Fatima, a Catholic grade school in Potomac. My brother Mike and sister Alyson were at Fatima—Joe had graduated and was in high school at Loyola Prep, an all-boys Jesuit high school— and I was familiar with the horror stories of nuns torturing them with ruler beatings, verbal abuse, and Marine Corps discipline. If I had a discipline problem, it would be fixed soon enough.

At Fatima I came under the charge of Father Paul, the pastor, as well as the nuns who taught us. Father Paul was a young priest with dark hair he kept slicked back and the body of a middle-weight boxer. He had been a champion wrestler in high school and college, had grown up in Washington, and knew every family in the parish personally. The kids loved him. As an athlete, Father Paul always expressed himself physically. When we got our report cards, he would stand in the front of the room to hand them out, and we got a small hug of congratulations or a squeeze on the shoulder if we needed to bring our grades up. If he saw you acting up, he would sneak up behind you, put you in a headlock, and rub your scalp with his knuckles before doling out the punishment.

"I think you're a wise guy," he would say sarcastically, rubbing his fist into the top of your head. "And you know what wise guys do when they're caught throwing rocks at girls? They write a five-thousand-word essay on the tragic consequences of violence."

Although Father Paul was cool—and it was after Vatican II,

the council that had liberalized the church—Fatima still had its share of authority figures who believed that the answer to every problem was a sharp rap on the knuckles. One such person was Sister Kate, the principal. Sister Kate was old-school Catholicism, from her full habit and 1950s catwoman glasses to the rubber stamps with angels on them—"Excellent" (a smiling cherub with hands pressed together in prayer) to "Poor" (a frowning, disappointed angel with eyes cast downward)—that she used to grade our homework assignments. A dowdy woman who looked like Icabod Crane, Sister Kate was perpetually tense and seemed always to be in the midst of an anxiety attack. Loud noises made her jump, and her emotions always ran to the extreme. If she was happy—which was rare—it was resplendent delight; if she was angry, it was pathological rage.

It was from Sister Kate that we learned to call each other by our last names. "Hey Judge," she would bark, "say one more word and you're staying after school." My fellow classmates weren't Karen, Jim, and Kathy—they were O'Neal, Murphy, and Kavanaugh. We also learned to walk in lines to go anywhere, to wear ties, and to address the priests and nuns as "Father" and "Sister." We were like raw recruits, and Sister Kate was the drill sergeant.

Between Father Paul's knuckles and Sister Kate's threats, I fell in line with the other kids, wearing my navy slacks and tie, sky blue button-down shirt, and behaving in class. I rarely saw anything but happy angels. I also became very religious. That might seem like an obvious development for a student in a Catholic school, but to many of the kids the faith was like eating vegetables—something you had to live with, but not that big of a deal. For me, however, the life of Christ was so charged with beauty and mysticism that it affected my body as well as my soul. In the warm spring days approaching Easter, during the Stations of the Cross, I would shudder with the ineffable power of Christ's slow ascent up Cavalry, and on Good Friday at three o'clock, the hour of Christ's death, I would stay still and silent, too awestruck with the power of God to even move.

My year was broken up according to the Catholic calendar. Fall, when the suffocating Washington humidity gave way to cool breezes and shorter days, meant not only Halloween but All Saint's Day. December, of course, meant Christmas. Early spring brought Lent, when we would give up something to prepare for Easter, the greatest feast day of the year—the "Solemnity of Solemnities." May 1 was the May Procession, another rite the church lifted from paganism. During the May procession, we would all march around the school before coming to a halt at the statue of the Virgin Mary in front of the church. There we would crown the Queen of Heaven with flowers.

For my first few years at Fatima, most of my teachers were

like Sister Kate, and I managed to stay out of trouble and get decent grades. We had parties and put on plays. My brother Mike, who would become an award-winning actor, always had a starring role. I grew close with my sister, who was two years older and a great basketball player. While Joe and Mike were so much older than me that we didn't have much in common, Alyson and I knew a lot of the same kids. We liked the same TV shows—*Happy Days, Good Times*—and loved sports, whereas my brothers were more into the arts.

From the beginning, I wanted to follow in my father's footsteps and become a journalist. While my classmates had fathers who were putting their time in as dentists and real estate agents, my father was having adventures in Borneo or the Sahara.

To me, any other kind of life would be a dull compromise. I taught myself how to type on my father's Underwood, and in fourth grade began to write poems and cover neighborhood events. The local paper, the Potomac *Gazette*, heard that I was a budding scribe and did a story on me (all mistakes are in the original):

Ten-year-old Mark Judge has all the earmarks of becoming a first-rate society columnist. Perhaps 'W' [a popular celebrity magazine] should sign him on at an early age, to secure his services for a later date. After all, the international society publication couldn't possibly go wrong, if Mark's latest wedding announcement is any criteria.

It goes as follows: "Janit Bushel became Mrs. Robert Martin today at the Potoamc Methodist church. The reseption toke [!] place at the Bethesda Navel Hospatil. The food was very good. At the reseption the band was called 'The Four Sharps.' The wedding started at 11:00 and ended at 2:30 to 3:00. Mr. and Mrs. Busel were very happy. Philles Judge was crying at the wedding. 'It was butiful' She said. . . ."

"He reports on everything," Phyllis Judge said about her son, a fourth grader at Our Lady of Fatima school. "He has just taught himself to type and his mind goes faster than his fingers."

Bolstering my interest in journalism was my discovery, abetted by my father, of literature. My father was introverted and difficult to please, but I knew that he admired people who were learned. There were certain books he considered classics that were necessary to read if one was going to live a rich and full life. One of my father's most loved books was J. R. R. Tolkien's trilogy *The Lord of the Rings*. It was a form of initiation in our family to read the trilogy when we were kids. Hoping to impress my father, I read the trilogy when I entered the eighth grade.

The Lord of the Rings tells the story of Frodo Baggins, a small creature called a hobbit who lives in the imaginary world of Middle-Earth. Frodo comes into the possession of a magic ring that allows its wearer to disappear; however, Frodo discovers that it is a trinket of evil. The ring is the creation of Sauron, the Dark Lord who lives in Mordor, and over time it warps the spirit and will of the wearer, turning him into a megalomaniacal distortion of himself. The only way to destroy the ring is by dropping it into the Cracks of Doom in the Land of Mordor, a place not unlike Dante's Inferno. On the way to Mordor, Frodo encounters the most terrifying kind of peril, not the least of which being the nine Dark Riders or Nazgul, evil emissaries of the Dark Lord.

I was completely enchanted by Tolkien's tale. Its overtly Christian themes of good versus evil and the importance of self-sacrifice bolstered my Catholic mysticism, and it became the most relevant piece of art in my life. My favorite scenes were the ones with the Dark Riders. While to the unaided eye the Dark Riders appeared as men on horses dressed in black—"wrapped in a great black cloak and hood, so that only his boots in the high stirrups showed below; his face was shadowed and invisible"—when Frodo put on the ring, he could see underneath their coverings. "In their white faces burned keen and merciless eyes; under their mantles were long gray robes; upon their gray hairs were helms of silver; in their haggard hands were sword of steel."

When the Riders attempt to capture Frodo, they cry out to him: "Come back! Come back! To Mordor we will take you!" It never failed to send a chill down my spine.

Reading *The Lord of the Rings* inspired me more than ever to keep writing. In addition to writing poems and articles, I began writing a book—a horror story about a man-eating shark that was heavily inspired by *Jaws,* one of the biggest movies at the time. My parents and teachers saw my interest in writing as a sign that I was destined to follow in my father's footsteps.

Unfortunately, in eighth grade my disciplinary problems soon overtook my literary ambitions, as well as my deep religious mysticism. My best friend at Fatima was a hyperactive red-haired Irish boy named Seamus. Seamus and I had become friends in first grade, and for most of our years at Fatima—when Seamus was unable to prevent his mother from giving him medicine (we called them "calm pills") to control his hyperactivity—we managed to be, if not perfect angels, almost as well-behaved as the rest of the class.

However, when we got to the eighth grade, Seamus revolted. His mother gave him the pills to take, trusting that he was old enough to monitor himself, and Seamus would make it a point to toss the pills out the window when no one was looking. As a result, Seamus became a cyclone of trouble. He farted in Mass—a ploy guaranteed to make me wet my pants from laughing—shot notes to girls when the teacher wasn't looking, and wandered off school grounds during recess. As his best friend and someone with a similar, seemingly innate penchant for mischief, I easily followed his lead. We became the twin terrors of the school. My grades began to plummet. My parents, though concerned, weren't about to panic. I was getting Cs, which wasn't failing, and they trusted that I could pick things up. They trusted, that is, until what I still think of as "the pens."

Because we didn't care about schoolwork, Seamus and I never had any pens. This annoyed our classmates, who were always loaning out their Bics to us just to watch them disappear by the end of the day. After months of supplying us with what seemed like bushels full of pens, they finally cut us off. We would have to buy our own.

One morning before recess, Seamus had a bright idea. We would stay indoors, and while everyone else was out playing, we would help ourselves to their pens.

It worked like a charm. While the other kids were on the playground, we simply circled the room and lifted all the pens off all the desks. By the end of recess, we each had a fistful of every imaginable kind of pen—green pens, red pens, cheap pens, silver pens with the kid's initials engraved in the side.

When the rest of the class came back from recess, we sat back and watched as twenty kids went through the exact same motions: they would reach for their pen, find it missing, bob their heads from side to side to search the floor, then start filing through their desk and checking their pockets. The most hilarious thing was that no one caught on that anyone else was missing a pen. They were all searching for their pens, totally oblivious to the fact that everyone else in the room was doing the same thing. Finally, kids began scurrying back to their lockers to fetch replacements.

It was too rich not to do again. The next day, we pulled the same stunt, with the same results—except now we had collected forty pens.

For the next two months, we lifted pens. We used an empty locker for safekeeping, and to try not to appear too conspicuous, we cut our operation down to two or three times a week. After eight weeks the locker was stuffed.

Our downfall was caused by the same thing that ensnares hardened criminals—greed. Although we had so many pens in the locker that it was no longer possible to open it all the way without setting off an avalanche of pens, Seamus could sometimes manage to hold the locker open a crack and slip a pen through. One morning during recess he did this, but then couldn't get the locker shut again. A pen was jammed into the hinges, and he couldn't get it out without letting up on the door. It had reached critical mass. Like the little Dutch boy with his finger in the dam, he could neither move nor stem the potential tide. He stood there, holding his weight against the tide and waiting for someone—hopefully me—to come along.

Finally, someone did—Sister Kate.

Although Seamus tried to look nonchalant, Sister Kate could sense that something was wrong.

"Seamus? Are you stuck or something?"

"Uh, no," he said, then peered into the locker. "I'm just looking for something."

"Well then open the door more than a crack."

Seamus looked at her helplessly. Sister Kate suddenly realized there was something in the locker that she wasn't supposed to see.

"Step away from there, Seamus."

I was in science class when Sister Kate came to get me. I knew right away that I was in serious trouble about something, and when I saw the entire floor of the eighth-grade hallway covered with pens, my chest tightened with fear.

"We've already called your father," Sister Kate said as we went down to the principal's office. "He's leaving work early to come pick you up."

I felt the blood drain out of my face. *My father was coming?*

"Oh, yes, you've done it now," she said, noticing my reaction. "Giggling during Mass is one thing. Even the time you boys

tried to crawl through the ceiling from the boys to the girls bathroom was almost understandable. But this is different. This is
theft." She spat the word out as if it tasted bad.

About a half hour later, my father came into the office
lobby. He was so angry he didn't even look at me. He went into
the office and spoke with Sister Kate for a few minutes, then
came out and led me to the car. I got in the backseat.

"Well, you are *out,*" he said, his voice tremulous with rage.
"You're expelled. Out. *Finished.*"

I averted my eyes from his in the rearview mirror.

"Good God, Mark, what are we going to do with you?"

I didn't speak.

When we got home, I went up to my room. I heard my
father talking to my mother, who was crying. My mother always
came to my defense no matter what, but this was hard for her to
take. I had been caught red-handed, and Sister Kate had told my
dad that after all the trouble I had been in, the stolen pens were
the last straw. She claimed that it pointed to a deep pathology,
maybe a budding kleptomania that should be treated.

My dad started making phone calls. He was calling all the
Catholic schools in the area to see if he could get me in someplace.

After about an hour, he got a call from Father Paul. Sister
Kate had overreacted. I wasn't expelled, just suspended. I also had
to write a five-thousand-word essay on the meaning of theft.

After hearing the news, my father opened my bedroom door. "You just dodged a bullet," he said.

By the end of the night, the pens were forgotten. One of my parents' rules was that you didn't go to bed angry, and they applied it to themselves as well.

Unfortunately, my troubles were just beginning. For reasons that had nothing to do with Seamus, Sister Kate, or how I was raised, I was a potential alcoholic. And I was about to take my first drink.

chapter

Crossing the Line

IF I ENTERED FATIMA A BUDDING MYSTIC, I CAME OUT APATHETIC about religion. Part of this was the result of my trouble with authority figures; somewhere amid all the detentions and suspension, God had lost the immediacy of Jesus on the cross. Instead, the creator of my universe was a huge, punishing, unreachable father figure—Sister Kate on a bad day.

Contributing to my apostasy were my parents, who had gradually stopped going to church while I was at Fatima. The Catholic priest and writer Andrew Greeley has noted that 90 percent of Catholics' feelings about their religion comes from whether they like their local parish, and my parents were no longer wild about Fatima. The main reason was money. The parish was expanding and claimed to need a new building to accommodate all the students—even though the baby boom was over and classes were actually getting smaller. As a result, Father Paul started talking about money during all of his homilies. We needed funds for the new Mother Seaton gym, he would argue, or for the expansion of the classrooms. Even after these things had been built, Father Paul continued to drone on about money. By the summer after my graduation, the Judges were C & E Catholics, only attending Mass during Christmas and Easter.

It was the summer after graduating from Fatima that I first got drunk. I was fourteen. It happened at Rehoboth Beach, a small beach resort down in Delaware about three hours from

Washington. I went there with Seamus, my fellow pen-swiper from Fatima. In just a week we would go our separate ways—he to public school, I to Loyola Prep, an all-boys private school.

It was the last night of the summer vacation, and Seamus and I left the house right after dinner. He told his mom we were walking over to a friend's house to play Ping-Pong, which was at least half-true—the house we were going to had a Ping-Pong table, but we were going there to get drunk.

On our way to the party we stopped to pick up Wendy, a girl Seamus had grown up with who also vacationed at Rehoboth. When we got to the house, a small wooden job that smelled like coconut tanning oil and pinecones, Wendy was still getting ready, so we waited on the front porch. While we waited, I started looking around. I always looked for copies of *The Lord of the Rings* when perusing someone else's bookshelf, hoping to find a kindred Tolkien fan.

Instead, I found a large book with a plain, dark blue cover without any marking. I curiously opened it up: "Alcoholics Anonymous," it read across the top of the page.

"You guys ready?"

It was Wendy. I almost dropped the book, then tried to shove it back on the shelf.

She saw me. "Oh, you've seen my dad's AA book," she said nonchalantly.

I just stood there, shifting my bare feet on the cool wood floor.

"Yeah," she said, smiling. "My dad's a recovering alcoholic."

I was stunned. Drunks were mean, dirty people, the ones you saw sleeping on the street. Unlike my dad, they didn't have distinguished jobs or live in the suburbs or vacation at the beach with their families. Wendy was revealing her father's moral decrepitude as if her father were a mechanic.

"Let's roll," Seamus said.

We left. I offered a feeble apology to Wendy, but she waved it away. "It's no big deal," she said.

The party turned out to be nothing more than a group of about six other kids our age and one older woman named Jean. Jean, who was in her twenties, was friends with Seamus's older brothers. She was our contact—the person who would buy the beer.

While we sat around waiting for her to get back from the liquor store, I felt a riveting excitement. We were about to get *drunk*. It was what happened to our parents when they went out to dinner or cocktail parties; they would leave the house responsible and buttoned-up adults and return home transformed into giggling, stumbling idiots. It was sexy, daring, and dangerous.

A half hour later, Jean came back, laying a cold case of beer on the kitchen table. Seamus pulled a beer off and passed it to me.

I opened it and chugged about half the can. It tasted bitter. I finished it and drank another.

About five minutes later, it hit me. I felt lighter, as if I was floating off the ground by a couple of inches. My head was warm. Suddenly, everything that happened around me was hysterical. Seamus belched so loud the windows rattled, and I laughed so hard I spit beer across the kitchen table.

"Jesus Christ," Jean said, jumping up from the table. "He's already drunk."

"Jean baby," I heard myself say. "Come over here and give me a kiss."

The others couldn't believe it. While they had also been drinking, my transformation was particularly dramatic. A few minutes before I had been the quiet friend of Seamus's that no one knew, and now I was blurting out everything that came into my head. I felt as if I had been charged with electricity.

Only years later would I understand what was happening. Alcohol, like other drugs, affects different people differently. Some researchers claim that in the brains of people with a chemical pre-disposition to alcoholism, the drug acts like an opiate, providing a mystical high not unlike heroin. This, they say, is why alcoholics can remember their first drink so vividly—from the start, it affects their brains differently. While everyone in the house was drunk, I was in orbit. Alcohol was a spiritual elixir, making me feel at ease with the universe and imbuing me with a sense of pure joy and serenity. I was wrapped in a warm cocoon of oceanic bliss.

After finishing the beer, we all headed down to the beach. It was dark, and you could only see the waves when they crashed white on the shore. A few of the other kids broke off into couples and wandered off into the dunes to make out. Seamus and I and Wendy sat down close to the surf and listened to the waves. I dug my feet in the sand.

"So where are you going to high school?" Wendy asked.

"Loyola Prep."

"Wow. That's a great school. Except there won't be any girls."

I leaned over and kissed her.

She didn't resist. Seamus got up and wandered off, and Wendy and I kissed each other some more. Then she took my hand and we lay on our backs and looked at the stars.

Nothing that had ever happened to me in church could compare to this. I felt like the classic hero Joseph Campbell describes in *The Hero with a Thousand Faces*. After being separated from home, the hero finds himself or herself in "a zone unknown." It is often a place of wonder, "of strangely fluid and polymorphous beings, unimaginable torments, superhuman deeds, and impossible delight."

●　　●

The next week, I began high school at Loyola Prep, whose neoclassical buildings, rolling hills, and golf course make it look more like a small college than a high school. It is a school steeped in discipline and tradition. Like every prep student since its founding in 1789, we dressed in coats and ties, said a prayer before every class, and went to obligatory Mass and confession. Of course, all of us were Catholics, so none of this was shocking.

What was, however, were my new teachers. As my first morning of my new classes wore on, I kept overhearing talk about Father Carmen, the headmaster who also taught art appreciation. Words like *psycho* and *nutcase* kept cropping up. Then someone came up and asked me if I had had the class yet. I told him no.

"Just make sure you're not late," he said.

By the time lunch was over, the warning had spread: at all costs, do not be late for Carmen's class. Unfortunately we only had three minutes in between bells to get to our next class, and the art building was in the main building—about three minutes across the quad from Cavanaugh Hall, where most of our classes were.

When the bell rang at the end of my first afternoon class, I was the first one out the front door of Cavanaugh. In what looked like a bizarre sporting event, about twenty of us "frosh" scampered across the campus dragging our bookbags behind us. We clambered into the art studio, a musty basement that was lined with pottery and covered with pictures.

At the front of the class stood a young, skinny Jesuit. He had dark hair and held a long wooden pointer in his right hand.

We tumbled into the desks and folded our hands. The room fell silent.

He watched us for a few seconds, his thin face so tense and scowling he looked as if he were in pain.

"Let's get two things straight right off the bat, gentlemen," he said. "Number one: when that bell rings letting you out of whatever class you have before this one, I want you to *move it*. I want you in your desks *before* second bell rings or you will be *out of here* for good."

His black eyes scanned the room. No one breathed.

"Secondly, there is a certain way I conduct this class. If I hear you tell anyone else that their project sucks or mention their mother, you should say hello to the wall because you're going through it. Is that clear?"

"Yes, Father."

"I CAN'T HEAR YOU, GENTLEMEN."

"YES, FATHER."

For the rest of the day, freshmen who had art class in the afternoon could be seen sprinting across the quad as if their shoes were on fire.

Father Carmen—who would loosen up considerably in the next few weeks, and who later explained to me that the first day of terror was just his way of establishing order, or "stepping on the bastards before they step on you"—was just one of a cast of characters that made up the faculty at Prep. There was Mr. James, the bald, four-foot English teacher with a gravelly voice so ripe for parody that he was the one teacher everyone could flawlessly imitate. Mr. Hartsby was the sixties radical who was studying for the priesthood; he would play rock songs by Devo, Elvis Costello, and the Who as part of his religion class. There were the older Jesuits, stoic, dignified men in black who were notorious for their scholarship as well as their prowess for emptying kegs, which were kept well-stocked in their residential cloister.

Indeed, it soon became obvious that drinking was one of the major forms of recreation at Prep. On Monday morning the upperclassmen would return from the weekend with stories about keg parties, girls, and hours spent in bars in Georgetown, a historic part of Washington that was known more for its bars than its monuments.

In the early 1980s, the drinking age was still eighteen. This was a leftover from the Vietnam era, when the age was lowered because of the obvious contradiction of denying alcohol to soldiers and nurses who were considered old enough to serve and die for their country. At Prep, seniors would often go directly from class to a bar. They would even drink with alumni at football games. Although I was still a freshman and not even sixteen, I was anxious to get into the drinking life and recapture the magic I had felt at the beach with Seamus.

For the first couple of years at Prep, however, I managed to keep straight. Despite the liberalization of American culture and morality since the 1960s, we were still upper-class Catholic kids who went to a Catholic school. Loyola, the oldest Catholic school in the United States, was heavy on tradition and discipline. The Jesuits made us stay at Prep until five o'clock every day to encourage us to get involved in extracurricular activities, and on the weekends our parents knew where we were all the time. When there was a dance or we wanted to go to the mall, they dropped us off and picked us up. It was like the 1950s.

I had made a new best friend at Prep, a kid named Shane Cuddy. Shane was a more subtle version of Seamus. Tall and blond, he loved to laugh and was an incurable wise ass, but he also was a good student. He would often follow, rather than instigate, trouble.

For our freshman year, Shane and I weren't as interested in drinking—although we both had older brothers and sisters who partied, so we knew it was in our future—as we were in girls. My mother would drop me off at his house and we would spend hours in his basement talking about girls. Shane had fallen for my next-door neighbor Becky Schmidt, a pretty blond who went to St. Catherine's, the all-girls Catholic school down the road from Prep.

The summer after our freshman year, Shane made his move. My mother and Becky's mother had decided to take Becky and me to Ocean City, a beach resort three hours from Washington, for a week, and we were each allowed to bring a friend. Becky brought her best friend Rene, a pretty girl with thin, narrow features and long black hair, and I brought Shane. We would be staying in a house with two beachfront apartments that were connected by a front porch.

Despite Shane's glibness and sarcasm, he was a sweet romantic and he pulled out all the stops with Becky. We took the girls to the boardwalk and went swimming with them, and every night we played cards together.

About halfway through the week, I was walking over to Becky's when I felt my foot catch on something. Instinctively, I yanked my foot up, only to collapse in pain. I had stepped on an enormous nail that was jutting out of the floorboard and ripped a gash in the bottom of my foot. I hobbled into the Schmidt's apartment. Seeing blood covering my foot, the girls started to get hysterical. Shane put me in a chair, and Rene began rubbing my shoulders while Becky got our mothers, who were back in our apartment. My mother and Mrs. Schmidt wrapped my foot in a towel and piled us all in the car for a trip to the emergency room.

By this time, I had completely forgotten about the pain.

Rene had her arm around me and wouldn't move. I was so stunned I couldn't think of anything else. If my wrap had fallen off, I could have bled to death and gone with a smile on my face. There was a girl, a pretty girl, touching me. I found myself hoping that it was a long drive to the hospital.

After they stitched my foot up, we went home. The whole way Rene was rubbing my back. I couldn't help but notice my mother smiling in the front seat.

That night, my mom and Mrs. Schmidt went out to dinner, and Shane saw it as our big chance to lose our virginity.

"You got it made with Rene, Judgie," he said. "Girls love that invalid routine." We were gorging ourselves on crabs, and Shane had a pile of empty shells that went up to his chin.

"The what routine?"

"The invalid routine, when you're hurt. My brother told me. When he played football in high school he broke his leg, and he *could not keep the chicks off of him.*"

"Really?"

"Right now, those girls are next door by themselves just *waiting* for us to make a move. If I were you, I'd claim that your foot hurt so much you couldn't get out of bed. She'll go in to see you, and then—shazaam!"

"Actually, my foot really does hurt, and I'm not supposed to walk on it. That's what the doctor said."

He spit out a crab shell. "Do it, then. Tell her you only have a week to live."

"I'll do it," I said.

He looked at me. "You're serious?"

"Bring it on," I said, trying to sound cool.

"Holy shit," he muttered. "What if your mom comes home?"

"I work fast, son," I said with exaggerated bravado.

He laughed, then clapped his hands and jumped up. "I'll go get her. Get back to the bedroom."

"Where are you going to be?" I asked.

"I'll take Becky for a walk down the beach."

I hopped down the hall and tossed myself on the bed. "I got this from my brother," Shane said, tossing a rubber onto my chest.

In the silence, I started getting nervous. *What if Rene actually would have sex with me?* I barely knew what to do.

A few minutes later Rene slowly came around the corner.

"How are you feeling?" she asked.

I tried to look sad. "It's a little sore."

She grimaced in empathy. "Didn't the doctors give you something for pain?"

"Yeah, but I don't want to take it."

She sat on the edge of the bed. "Can you walk?"

"Not really."

"I brought some cards," she said, showing me the deck. "I thought you might want to play."

I reached over and took her hand, then pulled her to me and kissed her.

When I pulled away, she blinked and smiled. "Boy you don't waste any time, do you?"

"Nope."

I was trying to sound confident, but I was so scared I thought I was going to barf. I drew her toward me again, but my heart was pounding so violently I held her slightly away so she wouldn't feel it.

We started kissing, and I gently rolled on top of her. Pain shot from my foot up my leg, and I grimaced.

"Are you sure you're okay?" she said.

"Yes," I said. I would have kept going even if someone had been amputating my foot.

We made out for a few minutes, then I reached for her chest. I figured I could breeze through that part then quickly move on to the final goal.

My hand wasn't even halfway there when she stopped me.

"Mark," she said incredulously, "I hope your not thinking this is going there."

"No, no," I said, trying to sound innocent. "I just thought, maybe—"

"You thought I'd feel sorry for you and give it up."

I rolled onto my back. "Where are the cards?"

● ●

A couple hours later, Shane came in. He saw us playing cards and gave me a side-eyed look. He thought we had been having sex for an hour and this was the aftermath. When Rene went home, I told him the awful truth.

"Yeah, things didn't go much better with Becky," he said. "Even though I told her I loved her."

"You *what?*"

"Yeah, I bit the big one. I told her I loved her. In Latin."

"What a minute," I said, letting it sink in. "You just told Becky Schmidt you loved her? In *Latin?*"

"*Amo te,*" he said.

"Holy shit," I said. "You've got to be kidding me."

"Hey, Father Carmen told us to try and use our Latin over the summer didn't he?"

I rolled onto my side and began laughing so hard I had to clutch the pillow for support. "Oh my God," I kept muttering. "You told her 'I love you' in Latin."

"You tell the guys at Prep and you're dead," he said.

Naturally, I did tell the guys, and Shane told them about my striking out with Rene. For a few weeks we were laughing stocks, but nobody had expected either one of us to score. We were Catholic boys hitting on Catholic girls from very conservative families and so young we probably wouldn't have known what to do had they let us go all the way.

●   ●

Unfortunately, the Irish-Catholic tradition couldn't completely shield us from drugs, particularly alcohol. Indeed, drinking had always been a part of our Irish-Catholic culture. When my sister turned eighteen in 1980 my parents threw her a party and thought nothing of it when a few of her friends got so drunk they had to be put to bed. By that time my brothers were both off in college studying English literature, but when they came home they would spend their vacations going to bars and parties with their prep friends.

None of our parents seemed to mind this, as long as the drug was alcohol, which many of them were addicted to. However, the idea of marijuana sent my parents into orbit. This had become evident in the mid-1970s, when my brother Joe had gotten caught selling dope. My father picked up the phone one night and accidentally heard Joe arranging to sell dope to another Prep student.

It was the only time my father physically hurt one of us. After overhearing the conversation, my father went up to Joe's room and closed the door. Suddenly there was a loud bang, as if someone had thrown a brick against the door. Except it wasn't a brick. It was Joe's head. My father—who, ironically, was drunk—so despised drugs other than alcohol and the whole drug culture that he was going to make sure we never got near it, even if it meant putting our heads through a wall, which is what he had done to Joe.

Afterwards, my father came back downstairs and silently went into his den. None of us, including my mother, dared to even move.

Of course, if Joe had been caught drunk, he wouldn't have gotten punished. Alcohol and faith were the glues that held our community together, and there was simply no way of getting through adolescence without at some point trying both.

My immersion into alcohol began at the end of my sophomore year, during beach week. Every year when we let out for the summer—because we didn't observe non-Catholic holidays, our school year was about a month shorter than the public schools—all the kids from Catholic school would pilgrimage down to the Eastern Shore for a week-long bacchanalia of drinking and sex, or at least attempts at sex.

We had the perfect arrangement. One of our classmates, Denny O'Neal, had gotten his parents to sign a week's lease for an oceanfront beach house in Ocean City, Maryland. However, the O'Neals had signed with the stipulation that there was going to be a chaperon there. What most of our parents didn't know was that the chaperon was Shags, Denny's eighteen-year-old brother. Shags was an assistant football coach at a Catholic grade school, and he loved two things more than anything else: beer and chewing tobacco. He was chunky, with a full, round face that was fish-belly white. He looked as if he had just stepped off the boat from Ireland.

As if having Shags as a chaperon wasn't enough, Becky had rented the beach house next to ours with some of her friends from St. Catherine's, and there were girls from Visitation, another Catholic school, in the house on the other side. We were going to be flanked by girls.

For Shane and me, the party started early. Shane's older sister Katy and her boyfriend John were also going down for beach week, and they offered us a ride. According to Shane, they were going to buy us beer and we could get drunk on the way down. The trip down to the Eastern Shore is broken into two parts—one hour to get to Chesapeake Bay, then two hours to Ocean City. Stretching more than a mile from end to end, the bridge offered a daunting and spectacular view of the Chesapeake Bay, and as we passed, Shane and I pressed our faces against the windows. The sailboats below looked like white pebbles dotting the floor of blue.

We got to the other side, and Katy's boyfriend stretched. "Man, I could use a beer," he said.

Shane and I both sat up.

"Pull over at the next place," he said.

Katy stopped at a roadside store. She went in and emerged with a case of beer.

I looked at Shane, who was sitting on the edge of his seat. We were like a couple of puppies at feeding time.

"I know you guys have been waiting," Katy said, "so here you go." She tossed two six packs over the seat.

We snatched up the beer. I drank the first one straight down, then settled back with the second. Then I had a third and a fourth. Within an hour, I had downed a six pack.

I woke up almost an hour later. For a second I didn't know where I was. My clothes were damp and sticky with sweat, and I had to piss so badly I could barely lift my legs. My ears rang.

I sat up.

"You better stop," I said.

I looked down at Shane. He was passed out, curled up in a ball on the seat with six empty beer cans at his feet.

"I'm serious," I said to Katy. "You have to stop or I'm gonna piss in my pants."

Katy pulled over to the side of the road. When the wagon jolted to a stop, Shane groaned and sat up.

"Shit, are we there?" he asked.

"About twenty minutes," Katy said.

"I have to pee," Shane said.

We both climbed out. I tried to stand but my foot had fallen asleep, and I tumbled then collapsed in a heap on the ground. John and Katy laughed hysterically.

We had stopped by a field, and the only trees were a row of pines about a mile in the distance. I hopped a few yards on my one good leg, then unzipped my pants.

"Hey, get farther away," Katy said.

"My leg's asleep," I said. I was still so groggy I could hardly see. I bounced on my one good leg and tried to pee straight. Cars honked as they drove by.

"Boy, you studs can really hold your liquor," Katy said.

A short time later, we pulled into Ocean City. Katy and John dropped us off at our house on 42nd Street, then left for Rehoboth, the resort thirty miles from Ocean City where she and her boyfriend were staying.

We were the first to arrive and didn't have a key to the house. We began wandering around the house looking for a possible way in. Shane started climbing the porch when someone called to us from the house next door.

"What the hell are you guys trying to do?"

It was Becky. She and four of her friends were sitting on their front porch.

"We're locked out until the other guys get here," Shane said, slurring his words.

"Oh my God," Becky said. "You guys are drunk."

"We had a few cocktails on the way down," I said.

The other girls peered down at us and started to giggle.

"Come on up," Becky said. "You can wait here until the other guys show up."

We climbed up to the porch from a wooden staircase on the beach. Becky tried to introduce me to her friends, but I was still too drunk to pay attention. I just wanted to go to sleep. I went into the house and landed on the sofa.

I laid my head on the pillow and began to lose consciousness, but not before realizing that I had entered a magical new world. A few hours earlier I had been at home, constrained within the parameters of parents, school, and church, but suddenly everything was different. After crossing the bridge—both literally and symbolically crossing into a new world—I had entered a new consciousness, and alcohol had been the vehicle. I was in a place where the unthinkable—like an attractive girl casually inviting you into her house, a house with no parents—was possible.

That night, the rest of the guys arrived. There were twelve of us staying in the house: me, Shane, Denny, Shags, a kid named Corey Joyce who was the biggest troublemaker in our class, and a few other prepsters whom I didn't know that well but who, during the week, would become my best friends. As the guys arrived, I felt an uncontainable excitement building. The anonymity of the suburbs had been replaced by a community of kids living feet, not suburban miles, from each other. Instead of being the black sheep in a family of achievers and the son of a drinking and distant father, I was a member of a new family.

The first thing we did was throw a party. We sent Shags out for beer and sent word to the houses on either side that we were having some people over. By ten o'clock the house was filled with girls. We blared AC/DC, the Who, and the Clash from the stereo, and tried to look cool drinking the five cases of beer Shags had bought.

About halfway through the party, Shags called for quiet.

"I know everyone's excited to be here, and I'm glad you all are havin' a good time. However, there are just a few ground rules," he said, pulling a piece of paper out of the pocket of his bathing suit. With this, we showered him with empty beer cans.

"Come on, guys, I mean it," he said, deflecting a shot to the head. "I have some announcements. First of all, no driving drunk. You guys want to go anywhere, I'll take you.

"Second, I get my own bedroom, and I've already picked it. That's right, it's the nicest one upstairs, the one with the air conditioner."

More cans.

"Screw you guys too. Lastly, you guys want beer, I buy it. You're all under age, and I don't want to have to haul your ass out of jail for getting busted with some cheesy fake ID." He looked around to let this sink in. "All right. Carry on."

A cheer went up. Denny put on "Highway to Hell," and pandemonium broke out. Guys began slam dancing, tackling each other, and drowning themselves in beer. Becky and her friends were just as bad. The Catholic school community was very insular, and we had known most of these girls since we were in first grade. They were like sisters, and they indulged with as much gusto as any of us.

While chaos erupted, I went out on the porch to watch the moonlight on the shore. I drank deeply from my beer. I felt both numb and electric with feelings of love, excitement, and spiritual ardor. It was like with Seamus at the beach all over again.

The next day, the guys established what would become our routine. We got up in the morning and hung out on the beach until the early afternoon. Then we retired back to the second-floor balcony of the house and played quarters. Quarters consisted of trying to bounce a quarter into a glass full of beer, then, if you were suc-cessful, picking someone to drink. If unsuccessful, you could "chance," try again, and if you failed, you would have to drink.

After quarters we would take a nap—or pass out, depending on how long the game had lasted. At night we would have a party, go to a party, or visit girls at the other houses.

It soon became clear that every one of us was a smart ass, and next to quarters the most popular sport became abusing each other, either physically or verbally. If psychologists are right that boys show affection through aggression, we must have been deeply in love with each other.

One night after Shane took a shower, he went to retrieve his bathing suit from the balcony wearing nothing but a towel. As he stepped outside, I noticed that Becky and some of her friends were sitting on the balcony of the house next door. In one motion I snatched Shane's towel off and slid the door shut. He was locked out and completely exposed. Part of being in the group was the ability to respond with humor in the face of such abuse, and Shane was an expert. In his birthday suit, and faced with a wall of female faces gawking and shrieking and hooting, he simply began to flex like he was Mr. Universe.

We lit each other's underwear on fire, had beer fights, and barfed in the sink. A couple of guys took pictures of their penises, and when it became evident that one of the guys had a member

that slanted, we called him Slope. The only one who didn't partici-
pate with real gusto was Shags, who, as a chaperon, was trying
to retain some dignity. It was pure slapstick and never seemed to
end. One night during a party I decided to escape to the second-
floor balcony and catch my breath and hang out with Shane, who
was sitting up there. Someone had left a large glass filled with beer
on the wood floor, and as I stepped onto the balcony, I accidentally
kicked the glass over. There was a kid on the balcony below, and
the beer dribbled onto his head. Thinking he was under attack, the
kid covered his head and moved to retreat into the house. But not
fast enough. The glass, after rolling around aimlessly on the
second-floor balcony, rolled over the side and smashed on his head.

It almost knocked him unconscious. While Shane and I
leaned on each other to keep from falling over laughing, the kid,
dizzy and drunk, stumbled to his bed and passed out.

There were girls in and out constantly. Though I had always
been girl crazy, up until beach week it had all been minor league
advances—games of spin the bottle at Our Lady of Fatima, a few
stolen kisses at dances, and my failed attempt at sex the previous
summer. Now I had an opportunity to make some headway. Most
of the time everyone, including the girls, was drunk. If you could
breathe and walk at the same time, you could hook up with
someone. This did not mean going all the way—for the most part,
these girls held to the beliefs of their very conservative families—

but after a year spent in school without girls, heavy petting was virtually an orgy.

About halfway through the week, we were having a party when Shane leaned over and whispered to me. "One of Becky's friends likes you," he said. "She's been asking about you since you crashed in their house that first day. She's over there by the quarters game. Her name's Mary."

I looked over. Mary was pretty, with dark hair, brown eyes, and a deep tan. She wore a bright yellow T-shirt and red shorts. She was intently watching the game.

I walked over to her.

"So who's your favorite band?"

It was a stupid thing to say, but I was drunk and didn't care how clumsy my approach was.

"R.E.M."

I immediately liked her. Not only because I loved R.E.M.— who would go on to become huge but at the time were a fairly obscure group from Georgia—but because I could immediately tell that she was friendly. Unlike a lot of other girls, she hadn't looked at me like I was weird or had said something dumb. She was honest.

"I like the Eurythmics," I said.

"Yeah, they're okay. I can never tell whether that lead singer is a man or a woman."

We paused to watch Denny miss a shot.

"So how do you like St. Catherine's?" I asked.

"It's okay."

"Do you have a lot of classes with Becky?"

Shags scored a hit, then handed me the glass. I drank. If you were standing anywhere near a quarters game, you could get picked—even if you didn't want to play or weren't paying attention.

"So how do you like Prep?" Mary asked.

"It's cool."

"Do you know Bart O'Kavanaugh?"

"Yeah. He's around here somewhere."

"I heard he puked in someone's car the other night."

"Yeah. He passed out on his way back from a party."

Shags scored again.

"Mr. Judge," he called, handing me the glass.

I drank. "I'm going to go out to the beach before these guys get me completely hammered," I said.

"Want some company?" Mary said.

"Sure."

We walked out to the beach. It was completely deserted, and we sat on a rise just above where the waves ran up the shore.

"So what do your parents think of you being down here?" I asked.

"Well, they think the chaperon is a responsible citizen. We got a woman who's about a hundred years old. All she does is sleep."

I laughed. "Yeah, my parents think Shags is a saint."

"But even with a chaperon, my father didn't want me to come," she said. "You should have heard the speech he gave me about coming down here," she dropped her voice. "'Fifteen-year-old girls should not be alone at the beach.'"

"I don't think my dad even cares that much," I said. "He just sits in his den and drinks all night, then says something like, 'Why don't you read some books instead of playing sports all the time.'"

"God, my dad is the exact same way. It's like they don't want us to have any fun."

We sat quietly for a few minutes, listening to the waves.

"So Becky told me you live in Potomac," she said. "I live there too, about a mile from the village."

"God, I hate Potomac," I said. "There's never anything to do. I remember when I was little, I saw this book about New York in the 1940s—I think it was a book about jazz or something—and I just couldn't believe how cool everything looked. The buildings were so much prettier, and there were all these people in the street. It just looked like there was so much to do and so many people. Potomac is so isolated."

"I've never heard anyone talk about it like that. It's so

damned expensive, you'd think it would be the perfect place to live."

I thought for a few seconds. "Yeah, maybe I'm just a spoiled brat. I guess I should feel pretty lucky to be able to live in a nice house and neighborhood."

"Well, I don't know if that's everything. When things are going wrong and you have no place to go and get away from it, it doesn't matter where you live."

I looked at her, then leaned over and kissed her.

We rolled over in the sand, and she began sucking my neck. I reached for her chest, but she stopped me.

"No," she whispered.

We stayed on the beach for about an hour, until people started spilling out of our house onto the beach. Everyone was drunk, and a few people went swimming. Mary kissed me, then went home. I returned to our house. The party was over, but a few of the guys were up. When they saw me, they almost collapsed with laughter.

Jesus," Shags said, poking at my neck. "You lose control of a vacuum cleaner or something?"

I went into the bathroom. I had a hickey the color of a jellyfish and almost as big.

I didn't care. I would wear a bandanna around my neck or just lie to my parents. I was happy.

I was also already an alcoholic, although it would take years of heavy drinking before I would realize this and begin to understand the disease of alcoholism. I would later learn that alcoholism begins when the alcoholic first starts drinking—not later, as much of the culture believes. The distinction between people who are alcoholics and those who are not would become painfully clear: People who are not alcoholics can go through phases where they drink heavily for long periods of time, but can then go back to normal drinking or even quit. But the alcoholic, whose chemistry is different and often lacks basic knowledge of the illness, finds it impossible to cork the bottle.

And I was an alcoholic. When I got back to Washington, my drinking would only get worse. I had crossed a line and tasted the fun of the party life, and there would be no turning back.

chapter

No Turning Back

THE SUMMER AFTER BEACH WEEK BROUGHT MANY CHANGES TO MY life. My brother Joe left for graduate school in Virginia and became seriously involved with Marianne, a med student whom he would eventually marry. Mike and Alyson were also both away at college, so the house was pretty quiet.

Despite feeling a little lonely, I was glad to have the place to myself. I had never been that close with my siblings, the result more of being the youngest rather than any animosity; by the time I was a teenager and ready to cultivate adult friendships, most of them had already gone on with their lives. Like many siblings, we knew each other, but not well. Besides, it seemed as though I only saw them at the worst times—Thanksgiving, after I had bombed my midterms, or Christmas, after I had received a wretched report card.

Although seemingly it would have been fairly easy for me to get good grades—I had scored high on enough standardized tests—I had the worst study habits of anyone I have ever known. Years later I would be diagnosed with attention-deficit disorder, but at this point I only knew that I had a difficult time keeping still and studying. My parents, possibly tired from raising the other three kids, never stayed angry long when I failed a course—in fact, they only tried to help, offering me tutors when my grades sank. They knew that I had a new group of nice Catholic friends and a girlfriend, Mary, and they never lost faith that I'd come through.

However, despite my frustration over getting low grades, I had more important concerns, namely girls and partying. A lot of guys in high school had relationships with women that were based primarily on sex—when you're a teenager lust just seems to drive out everything else—but Mary and I actually became good friends. (This is not to say I wasn't obsessed with sex, but Mary wasn't ready for it.) We talked on the phone every night and opened up about the troubles we were having with our fathers. Hers was overly strict, blowing up when she came in twenty minutes past curfew. Mine drank too much and, when he wasn't drinking, didn't seem to care what I did. Therefore, I took to doing what I pleased.

When I returned to Prep for junior year, drinking became a pleasure central to my life. Denny, Shane, Mary, her friends, and I started going to keg parties on the weekends, and if there wasn't a party, there was Georgetown. An elegant neighborhood of expensive colonial row houses on a rise just above the Potomac River, Georgetown is one of the oldest places in Washington. For high schoolers from all over the Washington area, Georgetown was also party central. While the back streets were red cobblestone and freshly painted homes, M street, the main strip through Georgetown, was a noisy bustle of stores and a bar on every block. There was only one minor problem: The drinking age in Washington was eighteen, and we were all seventeen.

To get around this, we did what has become a rite of passage in modern America—we got fake IDs.

There were two ways of obtaining a fake ID, one easy, the other incredibly high risk. The first way was simply to make one. I discovered how one afternoon while I was working in the yearbook office. Denny was one of the editors of Prep's yearbook. He had also become something of a legend around Prep when word got out that he had recently gotten a part-time bartending job in Georgetown by lying about his age. Denny was fearless and was always coming up with a scheme to rile up the administration. He and I were both interested in journalism and worked on the yearbook together.

One afternoon we were typing up some copy when I found a piece of plastic lined with black letters. The letters were all in various sizes, from headline-sized point to barely perceptible scrawling.

"What's this?" I asked, holding the sheet up.

"Just some stencil letters," Denny said, his face buried in a pile of photographs. "The publisher sends them to us so we can decide what size of type we want."

I put the plastic sheet on a piece of paper and rubbed one of the letters. It transferred onto the paper, and when I tried to erase it, it wouldn't come off.

"Man, this stuff really sticks," I said.

Denny's head popped up. "Wait a minute. What did you say?"

"These stencils. It's impossible to get them off."

Denny jumped out of his chair and examined the sheet. He pulled out his wallet, plucked his Prep ID out of the flap, and laid it on the table. Slowly he placed the stencil sheet over the letters on his ID, lining it up so the letters would correspond in size. Then he began to stencil.

A few minutes later, Denny had a fake ID. I gave him my driver's license and watched as he turned me into an eighteen-year-old.

"This is incredible," he said, squinting at his handiwork. "We have to try this out right away."

We jumped in Denny's car and drove to the small convenience store next to Prep.

"You go in," Denny said.

"Me? Why me?"

"Because you have a driver's license. It's better. All I have is this stupid Prep ID."

I got out of the car and went inside. It was a small store with only one register. There was a girl about my age ringing people up.

For about ten minutes, I wandered down the aisles, pretending to look over the rows of soup or paper towels while I was trying to work up my courage.

Eventually I worked my way over to the cooler in the back.

I grabbed a twelve-pack and then hustled to the front of the store. No one other than the check-out girl was there. I tossed the beer on the conveyor belt and pulled out my wallet.

She looked me right in the eye. "I need an ID."

"Oh, sure," I mumbled, trying to sound casual. I plucked out my license and handed it to her.

For what seemed like years she squinted at it, holding it inches from her face.

"Okay," she said, and handed it back. Then she rang me up.

When I got back to the car, Denny shouted, "It worked?" He snatched the bag out of my hand. "I can't believe it."

By the end of the week, Shane and the rest of our classmates were lining up to get into the yearbook office. We spent most of the next two weeks stenciling, and soon the store around the corner was getting heavy after-school business. The word spread to the other schools, and we expanded our services to the students at other Catholic schools in Washington. We did it all free of charge.

There was one kid, however, who didn't need our services—Corey Joyce. Corey had the worst reputation at Prep. He had only gotten into the school because his wealthy father had gone to Prep and was friends with Father Carmen. Corey had been in and out of reform schools and was one of the few boarders at Prep. The boarders lived on the grounds either because their homes were too far away to commute or because they had some kind of special need. Corey, whose parents lived in Washington but who wanted him under Jesuit supervision twenty-four hours a day, was definitely a special-needs case. Corey skipped Mass to smoke cigarettes—or, if he was caught and forced to go, would substitute lyrics in the hymns, changing "Shout from the highest mountain/Glory of the Lord" to "Jump from the highest mountain/Glory of the bored." He hid liquor in his room and always went around telling people he was an atheist. "Think about it, man," he said to me once during lunch. "Some dude that lived two thousand years ago dies and rises from the dead. It's just a story that was made up because people are such wimps about death."

When it came to fake IDs, Corey had us all beat. He had taken the high-risk road to acquire his fake ID, and as a result he was considered something of a folk hero. While the high-risk method of getting an ID didn't require the painstaking physical labor of creating one, it was a test of nerves that could rattle a hardened combat marine.

It involved going into the belly of the whale—the Maryland Motor Vehicle Administration. The MVA always looked like an army recruitment center: hundreds of people stood in long lines for hours waiting to be processed, and nobody was thrilled about being there.

Yet the system's very monotony presented an opportunity that was a fake-ID hound's dream. After you successfully took the tests, stood in the proper lines, and filled out the right forms for a license, you got your picture taken and signed the new license before it was laminated. However, between filling out forms and getting photographed, there was a long wait. You would sit in a large room with other applicants, and only when the MVA officer called your name would you get your picture done.

For those with the guts, this waiting period was the Achilles' Heel of the MVA system. The trick was to go with a friend who was of legal age and have him apply for a new license, claiming to have lost the old one. After presenting a birth certificate and filling out all the proper forms, he would be sent to the waiting room before getting the picture taken. Meeting him there would be his underage friend, who would respond in his place when the MVA official—often a Maryland police officer—called him for the photo and signature.

For anyone with the moxie, success of this quick-change resulted in a foolproof ID. It was actually the real ID of an older person, only with your face and signature.

Only Corey had pulled this off. As a result, he enjoyed the kind of freedom most of us dreamed of. He could walk into any bar or liquor store with his head held high and his hands steady.

The first time a group of us tried to use our IDs, we went to O'Rourke's, the bar in Georgetown where Denny bartended.

O'Rourke's was a real drinker's bar. It was in a two-story building and had three bars, one downstairs and two up. There were rickety wooden tables and a juke box in the downstairs bar, and only one beer on tap.

Even though Denny worked there, he couldn't guarantee that he would be working alone behind the bar, and it was usually the older, more experienced bartender who would card us.

A group of about ten of us, including Shane, Becky, and Mary, went down there on a Wednesday night when things were quiet. We walked past Denny without saying anything—if he said he knew us and then we got busted for fake IDs, he could lose his job. We got a table in the back and sat there quietly.

The older bartender, a large man with a neat white shirt, tie, and crew cut came over.

"IDs," he said.

We all tried to act surprised, then started fishing through our wallets and purses like it was a big imposition.

He collected up the IDs and slowly looked at each one. Then he went over to a bright little light by the bar—used to read credit card slips—and examined them further.

"We're screwed," Shane said.

The bartender came back to the table and handed me the stack of IDs like they were cards.

"What'll it be?" he asked

For a second, nobody spoke. We were so ready to get bounced that we were, at least mentally, halfway out the door.

"Uh, two pitchers of beer," I said quickly. "And make it fast, we're thirsty."

After that, O'Rourke's became a hangout not only for Prep students, but for all the Catholic kids we knew in the area. On some Saturday nights the place looked like a party at beach week, with about twenty Prep guys, Mary and all her friends from St. Catherine's, and girls from other Catholic schools. For the most part, our parents didn't seem to care. For one thing, we lied, telling them that when we did go out it was only to someone's house and we would have "one or two" at most. Second, most of our parents were drinkers, and they expected us to experiment a little.

Sitting in the smoke and the low, romantic light of O'Rourke's, I felt alive. I lost myself in the magic of alcohol, its ability not so much to blot out life as to bring it into focus, make it spiritual, magic. We would stay there until closing, then sneak into the house so our parents wouldn't wake up.

Around this time, I began to notice that not all drinkers are born alike. When I drank I felt hyperactive, yet focused and in control—at least until I had had so much, usually twice as much as anyone else, that I finally felt drunk—but everyone else was different. Shane would grow very quiet, his eyes squinting into tiny slits. Denny often became violent and antisocial, getting into fights or raging against his uptight parents before passing out. Becky had a very low tolerance and always stopped at two or three beers.

Of course, our parents and the Jesuits warned us against the dangers of demon rum, even while they were imbibing with frequent abandon. The cloisters at Prep where the Jesuits lived boasted a full bar, and our parents were always coming home well-lubed from cocktail parties. Still, we were underage, and the adults had to go through the motions of scaring us off the sauce. At one school assembly, Prep's headmaster, Father Carmen, brought in a priest who was a recovering alcoholic to speak to the students. Father Pat, a balding, heavyset middle-aged man, regaled the student body with the long story of his downward spiral into addiction. He had started drinking as a teenager in Detroit, and by the time he left the seminary he was drinking two bottles of wine a night. He wound up in a rehab for priests in Maryland and had been sober for ten years. Throughout most of his talk, we all cracked jokes under our breath or didn't pay attention at all.

At the end, however, Father Pat said something that made me take notice. "I know all of this is probably funny to you guys," he said. "And some of it is. Getting drunk, doing silly things—a lot of it is funny, and I admit that. But right now there's a guy in this audience who is going to have his first drink this year, and what happened to me is going to happen to him. He's probably muttering under his breath right now that I'm full of it, that he'll never become a boozehound. But it is going to happen. Statistics prove it. Father Carmen tells me you have 400 students here. Ten percent of the general population is addicted to alcohol. That means that forty of you are going to wind up like I did. I just want to say to those people that when it gets bad and you start drinking first thing in the morning to ward off the shakes, remember what I've told you. Don't be afraid to pick up the phone and call for help."

For a split second, I had a terrible thought: *What if one of those drunks were me?* I imagined myself lying by the side of the road in the worst part of town, vomiting into a drain. *I might be a trouble-maker,* I told myself, *but I'm no drunk. I have too much willpower.*

Father Pat thanked us, then stepped down. Father Carmen, who had been sitting by the podium, lept to his feet and warmly shook Father Pat's hand.

As well as being headmaster and art teacher, Father Carmen was Prep's drug czar, and he went about his duties with un-contained relish. Whenever there was a dance or a play at Prep, he would creep into the parking lot and rummage through back-seats looking for beer. Often he found it, and the guilty parties would have to report to the disciplinary committee, a group of faculty members that questioned problem students and decided their fate.

Of course, one place Carmen couldn't get at us was in our homes. When we didn't go to O'Rourke's, we took turns having parties. The word would get out that someone's parents were going away, and the other guys would pressure them into "popping," promising to help them keep things under control. This, of course, was a joke—I had seen houses destroyed by rampaging hordes of drunken teenagers, friends of the kid whose parents owned the house.

At the end of my junior year at Prep, my parents decided to go away for the weekend. By this time my brothers and sister were all out of the house; Joe had gotten married to Marianne and was living in Virginia Beach, Mike was living in the city and enjoying success as a stage actor, and Alyson was in school in Loyola in Baltimore.

I had the house to myself, but tried to keep the news from Shane, Denny, and the other Prep guys. I wasn't completely averse to having a party, but I had a healthy respect for the primary rule: don't announce too early. News of a party was like a deadly virus that had to be contained. If I spilled the beans too early in the week, the news would spread to Ocean City and the house would be overrun.

Unfortunately, my big mouth got the best of me. I was talking to Denny on Wednesday when he asked me if I had heard of anything going on over the weekend.

"Oh, I think we'll have something to do," I said.

He picked it up immediately.

"Wait a minute. Are you poppin'?"

"I didn't say that," I blurted. "There is no way that I'm poppin'."

"Your folks are away, aren't they? You're going to pop."

"No, that's not true—"

"You can't fool me, big guy. It sounds like you're poppin'."

I didn't say anything for a few seconds.

"Come on, killer," Shane said. "Pop."

"Cripes, okay," I said. "Just don't spread it around."

On Friday, Shane, Denny, Becky, and Mary showed up early to help me set up—or in this case, break down. We hid all of my parents' china and silverware in the attic. We moved all the good furniture into my father's den and locked the door.

Despite our precautions, I had a feeling I was in for an apocalyptic evening. The first sign came early. Shane and Denny were sitting in the family room drinking and waiting for the fun to begin when suddenly there was a loud boom in the distance and all the lights went out.

"Cool!" Shane yelled.

My heart almost stopped beating. I couldn't bring myself to

imagine what might happen: drunk revelers swarming through the house in the dark, smashing everything they came in contact with.

Sensing my panic, Mary clutched my elbow. "It's okay," she whispered. "Everything'll be cool."

We filed into the backyard and sat around the picnic table. Shane broke out a bottle of tequila and we took turns doing shots. I had to grit my teeth to hold the booze down, but in a few minutes I felt the warm glow creeping up my legs. Although I was getting drunk, I had a queasy feeling that even if the lights did come back, the blackout was an omen. Something disastrous was going to happen. I did another shot and tried to smile.

Just as I was about to lock the house and post a sign that the party was canceled, the air-conditioner fan in the backyard roared back to life, and the lights inside the house blinked on. Shane and Denny cheered and headed back inside. Outside, it was almost dark.

For the next hour, I felt like a stake planted on the beach as the tide came in. The flow of people started, slowly at first, a few shy girls clustered by the keg, then some more Prep guys—including bogus ID King Corey Joyce, who, probably just to prove a point, showed up with his own bottle of tequila. The backyard filled up, and then people started spilling into the house.

Right when I thought I might actually get lucky and just have a nice little party, the invasion began. Between eleven and midnight a steady stream of kids poured through the front doors. Cars lined up and down my street and beyond. I recognized seniors from Prep, and sophomores, then saw faces I had never seen before.

As space got tighter and tighter, I drank. The only way I was going to survive this was drunk, and because it was my party, I always cut to the front of the keg line.

By midnight, I was completely hammered. I took Mary's hand and we went to the top of the small hill in my backyard, away from the masses. We held hands and watched the swarming madness below.

"So when are your parents coming home?" she asked.

"Monday. I should have it cleaned up by then."

"It'll be all right," she said. "In a few weeks, you'll forget this ever happened. When it's over, we'll all help you clean the place."

I smiled. Mary always knew just what to say. For a second, I felt a surge of optimism. Yes, the party was out of control. But it would be over in a few hours, and then we would straighten things out. My parents wouldn't even know.

She turned my face to hers and kissed me.

"I love you," I said.

"I love you, too."

Just then, someone screamed my name.

I jumped to my feet. Shane came sprinting up the hill, out of breath.

"You better come quick," he said. "There's been an accident."

I raced down the hill after him. He led me into the house, then upstairs to the second-floor hallway.

The first thing I saw was the leg, hanging from a hole in the ceiling like a piñata.

For a second, I just stood there. It was like one of those times when people describe an accident, when everything begins to go in slow motion.

Then the leg moved, a jerky back-and-forth motion like its owner was being electrocuted.

I moved closer, and that's when I heard the voice.

"Goddammit, get me the fuck out of here! Where's the fucking door in this fucking place?"

It was attached to the foot. By now I was directly under the leg and could see that its owner, Corey Joyce, was still attached to it. He had gone into the attic, then kicked a hole the size of a footlocker in the ceiling.

I went nuts.

Someone helped Corey down from the attic and I grabbed for him, throwing a punch. I missed wildly, and Shane pulled me back.

"Jesus, man, I'm sorry," Corey said. "I couldn't see a fucking thing up there."

"What the hell were you doing up there?" Shane barked.

"I heard that there was booze hidden in the attic and went up to investigate."

Great. What he didn't understand—400 beers tend to cloud one's vision—is that in Potomac, attics were not accessible like the ones in the older homes. Ours was a new suburb with attics built for insulation, not human habitation, and when Corey climbed up through the square hole in the ceiling, he found himself in a big empty space with no light. Idiotically, he replaced the cover on the hole he had climbed through, plunging himself in darkness. Instead of feeling his way around the floor for the cover, Corey had panicked. He stomped against the floor with his foot, looking for an opening.

I covered my head in my hands. "Jesus, my life is over."

Just then, Mary came up the stairs. "Oh . . . my . . . God," she said, seeing the plyboards dripping down from the ceiling.

I went downstairs, unhooked the tap from the keg, and unplugged the stereo.

"OUT!" I hollered, shoving a group of people toward the front door. "Get out of my house! The party's over!"

"Hey man," a kid sneered, "get a life."

Before I could stop myself, I was on top of him. People screamed and we tumbled to the floor, but the room was so packed I couldn't even throw a punch.

Denny and Shane pulled me off. Luckily, the kid I had

attacked was smaller than me and was already gone.

"Get out!" I screamed. "The cops have been called and will be here any minute."

It was a bluff, but it got people moving.

After about a half hour, I had sent everyone home except for Shane and Denny.

Or so I thought. While I was upstairs reexamining the ceiling, I heard a noise in my parents' bathroom. It sounded like someone crying.

I went into their room, but the bathroom door was locked. I cupped my ear and listened. It was definitely the sound of sobbing.

I knocked on the door. "Hey, the party's over. Are you all right?"

The sound stopped.

"Come on, open the door."

I waited for a few minutes, then the door slowly opened.

She had long, curly black hair, but her face was hidden behind a fistful of tissue.

"I passed out," she moaned, rubbing her eyes. "And now my friends have gone."

"I'll take you home," I said. Even though I had been drinking for about six hours, I felt sober, even keen.

We went downstairs. Shane and Denny were sitting on the back patio finishing a bottle of tequila.

"What's your name?" I asked the girl.

"Laura."

"Guys, this is Laura. She got stuck here and I'm going to take her home. Try not to trash the place while I'm gone."

"I don't think we can improve on Corey Joyce," Shane said.

"Don't remind me," I said.

"So are your parents going to kill you?" Laura asked as we drove down Connecticut Avenue. She lived in Chevy Chase, the tony part of Washington where my father had grown up. Wary of cops I drove carefully, but it was past three o'clock in the morning and the streets were empty.

"I don't even want to think about it," I said. "My dad is going to *freak.*"

"He's pretty uptight, huh?"

"Not really. He's actually a real intellectual introvert and doesn't yell a lot. But when he gets a few drinks in him, he can be really nasty."

"My dad's really strict. He and my older brother used to fight all the time when my brother was in high school. But then my brother started playing football and they started getting along better."

"Your dad was mean to your brother just because he didn't play football?"

"Yeah. My dad was a big jock when he was in high school,

and he was kind of crushed when my brother didn't want to play sports. My dad kind of forced him."

"He *forced* him?"

"Kind of. I mean, he didn't say he was going to disown him or anything if he didn't play, he just kept pressuring him, you know, telling him how sports build character and everything."

"God, what a dick."

"Actually, it worked out really well. My brother rode the bench all season, but he and my dad started getting along really great."

"That's beautiful," I said sarcastically. More and more, my dad was looking good. So many of my friends had parents who drove them into sports or other things they didn't want to do. All my father had done was try to instill in us the magic of literature and learning. Listening to Laura, I suddenly felt lucky.

"Take a right on Tennyson," she said. "It's the fifth house on the left."

I pulled into the driveway. She lived in a large white colonial house with three floors.

"Good night," I said.

She looked at me. "Uh, do you want to come in for a beer or something? My parents are at the beach for the weekend."

For a second, I was too surprised to say anything. *It was three in the morning. My parents' house had been trashed. She wanted to have a beer?*

Then it hit me. *This girl wanted to have sex.*

I stopped the car.

In the back of my mind, I told myself I should just start the car, back down the driveway, and head home. I couldn't do this to Mary.

"Sure," I said.

We went into her house, then into the kitchen. Laura opened the refrigerator and pulled out two beers.

She had barely turned back around when I was on her. She moaned and put her arms around me.

"Let's go upstairs," she whispered.

We left the beers on the counter, and she led me up the stairs by the hand.

We fell onto her bed. She pulled her shirt off, then her pants. I followed.

It was over in a matter of minutes.

I rolled off of her and looked at the ceiling. Free of the drive of lust, the reality of what I had done, of everything that had happened, began to sink in. I had just plunged a dagger into Mary's heart. I would never be able to face her again.

"I'm a dead man," I said.

Laura mumbled. She was already half-asleep.

"My parents are going to disown me."

I got up and got dressed. Outside, a car down the street

coughed to a start. The sound pierced my soul, like the cock of the crow on Judgment Day. I had hoped that maybe time would stand still for me, that I could hide here. The starting car heralded a new day. Time would continue, and I'd have to face my parents and Mary.

I got in the car and drove home. If I could have, I would have started heading west and never come back.

When my parents got home and saw the damage, they were too shocked to speak. My father slowly walked around the house, silently examining disaster after disaster. There were burn marks on the living room table where people had put out joints, and most of the patio furniture was in splinters. The mailbox had been plowed over.

I didn't even ask about my punishment, and he didn't say anything. I just went about trying to repair the damage. I went out to the hardware store and bought a new hammer, nails, and screws, and helped my dad fix the patio furniture that wasn't beyond hope.

The following Saturday night I stayed home, hoping to get back in my parents' good graces. Late at night, I went downstairs for a midnight snack. My father was sitting at the kitchen table reading. He was drunk.

"Hey, dad," I said.

He didn't even look at me. "I want you to get a job," he said.

"Right now?" I asked. I tried to laugh and sound light-hearted, but I was frightened. He was drunk, and it was like dealing with a different person.

"This isn't funny, Mark. This summer I want you to have a job."

I felt myself get tense. Although I had seen my dad like this often, it was always unpleasant. He wasn't worried about me having a job over the summer. He just wanted to pick a fight. Still, I didn't fully appreciate the warping effect alcohol could have on the human brain, the way it turns people into monsters.

"I'll go out tomorrow and ask about some work," I said. I started making a sandwich. He just sat there watching me.

"Are you planning on going to college?" he finally said.

I nervously laughed. Despite the obvious, I would just keep pretending that he wasn't drunk.

"Of course," I said.

"I don't think you're smart enough to go."

I stopped making the sandwich and put the supplies back in the refrigerator. I knew that he wasn't going to leave me alone and that I just had to get away.

"You know," he said. "Your buddies are jerks. Staying out late," he growled, "going to bars. You guys think you're a bunch of hotshots."

I turned to face him. "But Dad, you did the same thing when you were my age."

He didn't say anything for a few seconds; he just played with his drink and watched me finish making the sandwich. I almost wished he would have laid down the law, issued an order, told me I was grounded for a week—some signal that he cared. But I knew he was just shitfaced and looking for a fight.

"I want you to read something," he said. He disappeared into his den, then came back holding a book. It was called *Washington and Baltimore,* a collection of short stories by Julian Mazor.

"I want you to read the last story in this book," he said. "It might help you. Because your mother and I don't know what we're going to do with you, Mark."

I opened to the table of contents. The last story was called "The Boy Who Used Foul Language."

"The writer lives in Washington. He's a recluse. He wrote some great stories for the *New Yorker,* but after he published this book in 1968, he disappeared. I've often wondered what ever happened—"

"Can we talk about this tomorrow?" I said. This was always my ace. I would agree with everything he said, yet ask that we talk about it in the morning. Of course, by then he would be sober and would have no interest in having such a heart-to-heart.

"I'm serious, Mark."

"I know you are, Dad. I'd just like to talk about it tomorrow."

"Your grades at Prep have not been great—"

"Dad—tomorr—"

The drink hit me in the face so hard that I tumbled backwards and onto the floor. I ran out of the room so fast I almost knocked him over, then down the stairs and outside. I shot down the street and out of the neighborhood, the air roaring in my ears.

I picked up a path that Seamus and I used to take. It ran through the woods and to the village. When I was too exhausted to keep running, I slowed down to a walk. I hadn't noticed before, but I was still carrying the book my father had given me. I kept to the path, the early summer night buzzing with the sounds of crickets and frogs. I imagined myself as Frodo in *The Lord of the Rings,* carrying the evil ring through the forest and toward Mount Doom. I was on the run from the Nazgûl, the servants of the Dark Lord who rode on winged creatures.

About an hour later, I got to the village. I sat on the sidewalk in front of the supermarket, wondering what to do. It was after two o'clock, and a phone call to any of my friends would freak their parents out and get me in trouble.

There was only one option and only one person I wanted to talk to—Mary. She lived about a mile away and had her own private line.

She answered on the first ring.

"Mary."

"Mark? Are you all right?"

"Listen, I'm up at the village. I had some trouble with my dad."

"Your dad? Are you okay?"

"Yeah, just the usual bullshit. But I need a place to crash."

"Hold on. I'll be right up."

A few minutes later, Mary pulled up. She took me back to her house, and I told her what had happened. She led me around to the back of the house and down a short flight of stairs to the finished basement.

"You can sleep on the sofa," Mary whispered. "Just don't make any noise or my parents will wake up."

I sat on the sofa. She sat next to me and started kissing my neck. We made out for a few minutes. I touched her breast, and she let out a little sigh.

Then I stopped.

"I can't do this," I said.

She backed away, surprised. "We're not doing anything."

"I know."

"And you know I'm not ready to have sex yet."

"I know."

"So what's the problem?"

The problem was obvious to me—Laura. Just being here was

a slap in Mary's face, and I shouldn't have been touching her. Worse, I was convinced that I was in love with Laura. She had completely given herself to me, unlike Mary and the other girls I knew.

"I guess I'm just tired," I said. "You know, the fight with my dad and everything."

"I understand," she said. She kissed me goodnight and went upstairs.

I lay down, then opened *Washington and Baltimore* and read "The Boy Who Used Foul Language." Mazor's writing was sublime. Set in the 1940s, it told the story of a young boy, John, who had gotten expelled from school for fighting with a boy who hurls a racial slur at John's African American maid. John was no angel, but he was a troublemaker with a moral center. At the end of the story, he knows he'll fight with the same boy again, but seems to rejoice at the prospect.

The message my father was sending by giving me the story to read was clear: I was a moral, decent boy, but could too easily succumb to forces that would ruin my life.

I reread the story, then started on another, falling asleep with the book on my lap.

The next morning, after Mary's parents left for church, she drove me home. I knew that I was safe because it was daytime and my dad had sobered up; however, when I got to the house my parents weren't home. They had gone for a drive in the horse country in west Potomac.

In my room, lying on my pillow, I found a note:

SORRY ABOUT LAST NIGHT—BOOZE TALKING

chapter

A Functioning Alcoholic

"LISTEN, MARY, I DON'T KNOW HOW TO SAY THIS, BUT I DON'T
think we can go out anymore."

The other end of the line fell so silent that for a second I
thought the phone had gone dead.

"Um, I met somebody," I blurted, anxious to fill the silence.
"It just happened really fast and I didn't mean to hurt you. It just
happened really fast. I wasn't even expecting it. I—"

"You met her at your party, didn't you?"

"Mary, please—"

"Tell me."

I waited, listening to the silence between us.

"Yes, I did."

"You had sex with her, didn't you?"

"I don't see what good this—"

"Just tell me."

"I just want to go out with her, okay?"

"You had sex with her, I can tell."

Her voice trailed off. She started to cry.

"I'm sorry," I said.

She hung up.

It was one of the dumbest things I had ever done. Mary and
I had a friendship and a foundation that might have even made it
possible for us to get married someday, and I had tossed it away.

Unfortunately, I was seventeen, and my hormones were

making all the decisions. While Laura and I didn't have much in common, there was one thing that made everything else seem irrelevant: sex.

And that summer we had the opportunity to have plenty of it. Laura's brother, the one who had played football, had moved into his own place in Georgetown, and both her parents worked during the day. For the entire summer, she had the house to herself, all day every day. I would come over to watch a little TV or play Ping-Pong, but we would always wind up in her bedroom.

Even when I was doing this, I knew that dumping Mary had been mean and callow. Mary and I had been friends, and no matter how hard I tried, I couldn't achieve the same level of comfort with Laura. I liked comic books, beer, and punk rock; she was into sports—particularly football—and fast, expensive cars like the Porsche her father owned.

In fact, Laura hated the car I drove, a black 1964 Volkswagen Beetle that had belonged to my father and was always on the brink of collapse. The first time Laura saw it her face suddenly went sour, and before I could kiss her she asked, "That's not yours, is it?"

This was part of the ugly side of growing up among affluent people. Many of the well-to-do Irish-Catholics in Washington were very conservative. While it was central to the faith to help the poor, and most of my friends and their parents cared more about your manners, sense of humor, and character than what kind of car you drove, there were also those whose main goal in life was to get as rich as possible and groom their kids to do the same. These were the people who had their children's future mapped out from the day they were born, from Fatima through the Ivy League and partnership in the best law firm in Washington. Laura was such a kid. Her parents were both attorneys, and they only let her date wealthy boys—and, if possible, ones who played sports.

The first time I met her father, I knew we would never get along. I came by the house one night to pick Laura up for a movie, and he was in the family room watching a Redskins pre-season game. He was about twice my size and in better shape, with a broad, mean face and crew cut. When he stood to shake my hand, I felt like a ten-year-old.

"So, you watchin' the Skins?" I said, trying to make conversation.

He grunted. "That damned Thiesman," he said. "He's got to learn to stop panicking and stay in the pocket."

"Yeah, I've heard that," I said. I had no idea what he was talking about.

"So Laura tells me you go to Prep," he said.

"That's right."

"So you must play for coach Clancy."

For a split second, I thought about lying and telling him I played football. Joe Clancy was Prep's football coach, and he had never had a losing season. Everyone Catholic and almost everyone else in Washington knew who he was. He was considered practically a saint.

"Uh, actually, I don't play football."

"Oh," he said. The temperature in the room dropped by about twenty degrees.

"Yeah," I said. "I'm more into soccer." It was a bald-faced lie, but I wanted to come up with something that would impress him.

It was the wrong move. He snorted, a smirk on his face. To this guy, soccer might as well be Ping-Pong.

"Well, at least I know you like girls," he said, giving me a light punch in the leg. He laughed loudly, and so did I. I felt like a twerp.

On the way to the movie, I told Laura what had happened.

"So why *don't* you play football?" she asked.

"I guess I just never thought of it," I said.

It was the truth. My brothers had been intellectual and artsy, and had always put down jocks as no-necked meatheads. I had been influenced by their position, even though Shane, Denny, and most of my friends at Prep were football players. Although I had played sports when I was younger and played them well—my Little League batting average was always over .300, and I was always one of the first picked for teams at Fatima—at Prep the interest had dropped off in favor of other interests. Like drinking.

"You should play this year," she said. "It would probably impress your father and win him back after that party you had."

I thought about this for a while; maybe she was right. Playing football meant that I would have practice every day until five o'clock, which would keep me out of trouble. Moreover, Shane, Denny, and the other football players always organized the best parties. It would put me right in the center of action.

When I told the guys I was trying out for the team, they laughed. Even they considered me a troublemaker who cared more about girls and partying than sports. But I didn't let their jeering dissuade me. I knew I was at least as coordinated as these guys—in many cases much more so. Not that my ability or desire would have anything to do with it. Most of these guys had been playing football since freshman year. Coach Clancy had a pretty good idea of who was going to play where, and it would be all I could do just to get noticed.

Everyone at Prep knew that while screwballs like me who spent many afternoons in JUG—"Justice Under God," the Jesuit moniker for detention—could often play certain noncontact (read: wimpy) sports like baseball or swimming, there was a clear demarcation when it came to football. At Prep, football was held in divine reverence. Guys would start preparing themselves for the varsity while they were sophomores or even freshmen, although only upperclassmen got to play. It was completely unheard of for someone who had never played organized football—and who was only 5' 8" and 150 pounds—to walk on senior year and make the team, especially if that person's main activity in life was serving an addiction to alcohol.

It was the summer before senior year, and by now, even though I wasn't drinking every day, I was completely hooked. Going a week without getting drunk was unthinkable. I was spending between four and seven nights with the gang, either at a party or at O'Rourke's. Because we were going to be seniors, our parents gave us tremendous slack. We were pretty much left alone to do what we wanted, when we wanted.

Of course, I didn't consider my drinking an addiction. I didn't think I fit the stereotype of an alkie, which was linked with harsh scenes of debilitation: homelessness, tremors, broken nose veins, and hospitalization. I later learned that while all of that can be part of the illness, many alcoholics, like other drug addicts, can function—and function well—despite the fact that they are addicted. They don't miss a day of work and are never late for appointments. Indeed, in the early and middle stages of the illness, alcoholics seem to be blessed by their super-human tolerance.

Furthermore, the drug can act as a normalizing agent, curing the very problems that it has caused, much the way nothing cures a nicotine fit like a cigarette. In the classic film *The Lost Weekend,* the lead character, an alcoholic, tries to correct a bartender who thinks alcoholics drink in the morning simply because they like to. "You just don't understand," the alcoholic, brilliantly played by Ray Milan, pleads with the bartender. "It's medicine."

Of course, alcoholics also get into all kinds of trouble because of their drinking. When they supersede their own tolerance, they suffer catastrophic hangovers. These can make getting through the day an Olympic event. This was never more evident to me than when, to raise money for football camp, I spent a few weeks working as a bag boy at the local supermarket.

My job was simple. People would leave their grocery baskets against a rail in front of the store, then pull their cars around. I would then sling their groceries in the car, sometimes get a small tip, and then wait for the next car.

It was a nightmare. Invariably I would be hungover—or still drunk—when I got to work at seven in the morning, and I spent most of the first hour just trying to hold myself together. I had stopped eating breakfast a year earlier, so I didn't have to worry about trying to keep food down after a bender, but sometimes I was so toxic from the alcohol that I would have the dry heaves. Luckily the bathroom was a private room in the back of the store, and I often managed to recuperate there unnoticed. Or I would sneak into the patch of woods behind the store and rest for an hour, usually getting back before anyone noticed.

To get away with staying out till all hours, I would often spend the night at Denny's house. Denny had eight younger brothers and one younger sister, and the family lived in a gigantic house about four miles from me in Potomac. For most of the guys at Prep, the O'Neal house was a home base. They had a pool, a patio as big as some people's houses, and a backyard the size of a football field. Their house was so big that ten of us could stay over after a night out. After we got up, Mr. O'Neal would fix a huge bacon and egg breakfast, and we would lounge around exchanging war stories—who got lucky, who didn't—while kids raced through the house and crawled around our ankles.

. But the O'Neals were perhaps most famous for their parties. Twice a year, at Christmas and at the end of the summer after football camp, catering trucks would pull up to their house and unload enough supplies for an army. Pounds of fancy sandwiches, shrimp, and chocolate-covered strawberries, as well as kegs, crates of wine, and booze were moved into the house. Bartenders and cooks were hired. And all their kids, from the youngest to the oldest, invited their friends over. These bashes were always among the highlights of the year. At Christmas, it was a chance for us to get away from our families; at the end of the summer, it was a celebration of the football players making it through camp.

Before the shrimp and kegs, of course, I had to live through camp. For two weeks we would all stay at Prep, using the dorm rooms that belonged to the boarders—who were on summer vacation.

On the last weekend before camp, I broke the news to my dad that I was going to try out for the team.

He looked at me with complete disbelief. "You're going to get killed," he said.

His response was exactly what I *didn't* expect. I thought that being the son of a professional athlete, he would be thrilled that I was doing something other than sitting in JUG every afternoon. I also noticed a rare tone in his voice. He wasn't angry; he was genuinely worried. He knew how big some of my friends were and thought that two weeks of full-contact football with them would land me in the hospital.

"I'll be fine," I said.

He went back to his drink and didn't say anything else.

That night, I met Shane, Denny, and some of the other players at O'Rourke's for a final blowout before two weeks of hell under coach Clancy.

For the first round, I ordered a pint of beer and a shot of bourbon.

"You better be careful," Shane said. "We report in two days."

"Yeah," added Denny. "You don't want to be puking the first practice."

"Screw it," I said, and did the shot. It was going to be my last binge for two weeks, and I wanted to go out with a bang. I ordered another shot, and Denny shook his head.

"You gonna pour him home tonight?" he asked Laura.

She made a face. "God, I hope not. He's supposed to spend the day with me and my parents tomorrow."

Cripes, I had almost forgotten. Her parents had invited me over for brunch the next day. Her father was starting to warm up to me since I had decided to go out for the team and wanted to talk about the new season.

"Are we going to stay here all night?" Laura said, more to the table in general than to me.

"Yes," I said, and ordered another shot.

Even though she was a party girl, Laura was getting sick of my drinking. Moreover, we liked different bars. She liked places with flashing lights and pounding music where the guys all wore cologne, and I always insisted on the dingy quiet of O'Rourke's.

I knew that making it through brunch with a hang-over would be murder, but I didn't care. I also didn't have any idea how dangerous doing shot after shot was. Up until then my drink of choice had been beer, and despite the fact that I was living in a culture of drinking, I was sadly misinformed about hard liquor. I had always assumed that it was just like beer only it tasted stronger.

I sat there and did four shots in a row, ignoring everyone telling me to stop. I was going to football camp and would possibly have my head separated from my shoulders, and I just wanted to drown the fear.

"You better ask for a stretcher," Shane said.

I ignored him, and ordered another.

The next thing I knew, I was lying on a bathroom floor. I was curled up in the fetal position with saliva running out of the side of my mouth.

I sat up and tried to open my eyes. Then I struggled to my feet and looked in the mirror. My hair was sticking straight up, and my face was chalk white and swollen. It looked like a bunched-up pillow. My T-shirt was soaked with sweat.

I took a long drink of water, then splashed some onto my face.

I slowly walked out to the hall. I was in a hotel or apartment building. I took the elevator downstairs and found myself in a hotel lobby. It was quiet and empty, and outside it was dark.

There was an old bald man sitting behind the desk, and when he saw me he started. I must have looked like the ghost of John Barleycorn.

"Excuse me," I coughed. "What time is it?"

"Three-thirty."

Holy shit. I was a dead man.

"Where am I?" I asked him.

"The Four Seasons Hotel," he said. Then he reached for the phone.

"You don't have to call security," I said quickly. "If you just let me call my friends, I'll wait for them outside."

He looked at me for a couple seconds, then handed over the phone.

I had to call home. There was no choice. I had no money left to get home, and I had no idea if the others were looking for me or not.

My mother answered on the first ring.

"Mark?" she blurted. "Is that you?"

"I'm sorry, Mom," I said, starting to cry. "I'm sorry."

"It's him," she said to my father. "He's all right."

I heard more voices in the background, including two I knew—Shane and Denny.

"Where are you?" my mother asked.

"At the Four Seasons in Georgetown. I must have come over here and passed out."

"Just hold still. Someone will be down to get you."

About a half hour later, Shane and Denny pulled up. None

of us said much on the drive home, but I could tell they were pissed. It was now Sunday, which meant that we were reporting to football camp in one day. The last thing they wanted was to be up all night. When I asked them what had happened, they said that at one point during the night I had just disappeared. They thought I might have gone home or met a girl and didn't worry too much about it. Then, at three o'clock, they got a call from my parents. I hadn't come home yet; was I at the O'Neals's? No. They thought I must have passed out somewhere or been killed. Denny and Shane came over to my parents' house and had barely sat down when the phone rang.

We passed through Washington and into the suburbs, and I felt fear tighten my chest. My father was up, and he was waiting for me.

When I walked through the door, my father was standing in the front hall. Expecting the worst, I backed away from him, retreating into the family room. I closed my eyes and started to weep.

He turned me to face him, then held me. "I thought you were dead," he whispered. I began to sob, burying my face in his chest.

"I'm sorry, Dad," I moaned. "I'm so sorry."

My mother came in and wrapped her arms around me.

"God, I'm so sorry," I wept.

They held me tighter. For all of our problems, they didn't deserve this. No one did.

Needless to say, I didn't make it to brunch the next day. When I called to cancel, Laura hung up on me. By then, word was all over town about what had happened.

● ● ● ●

On Monday morning, we reported to camp. It felt odd being at school in August, when the only other people around were the coaches and Father Carmen, who lived at Prep. Writer Gore Vidal once called Washington summers "Egyptian," and with good reason. When I got to Prep, I knew it would be one of those ninety-degree days. The towering oaks in the quad braised in the dead summer air, and it was so humid a haze hung over the practice field.

From the beginning, I felt like an idiot—not so much because I was afraid of being hurt, although that was certainly part of it, but because I didn't know so many technical things that the others took for granted. I quickly realized that if I was going to make it through camp alive, I'd have to accept that there was no such thing as a stupid question. I found Shane putting on his equipment and sidled up next to him, asking him everything from what size helmet I should use to how much water I should drink. With his help I managed to suit up.

I felt like a turtle with a shell that's too big. Rather than making me feel bigger and more powerful, the full football regalia left me feeling small and vulnerable. The pads were awkward and smelled like old sweat. I had a new appreciation for football players who managed to maneuver so gracefully inside the armor, making it look easy.

We took to the field. Although it wasn't even nine o'clock yet, the temperature was already approaching eighty. The vantage point inside my helmet made me feel as though I was in a tank preparing for combat. But the battlefield was missing one key player—Coach Clancy was nowhere in sight. We began to loosen up and play catch.

At exactly nine o'clock, the doors to the gym exploded open.

"Oh, this is a GOOD DAY TO DIE today!" Clancy roared. "A GOOD DAY TO DIE, BOYS!"

Everyone erupted into shouts and hollers, clapping their hands as if the Pope had just arrived. However, they weren't applauding Clancy—they were celebrating the fact that they were about to do something truly sadistic and dangerous: play football in ninety-degree weather. Like World War II paratroopers shouting "Geronimo!" before leaping, it was an absurd response to a ridiculous predicament.

I began to weakly clap, ruing the day I opened my mouth at the keg party.

"It's a GOOD DAY TO DIE, YESSIR!" Clancy bellowed.

Everyone fell into rows and began doing calisthenics, counting together like marines. Then we caught punts, hit tackling dummies, and ran a few plays.

"How's it goin'?" Shane asked.

I smiled. "This is easy."

He smiled. "It will be until after lunch."

After lunch, we retook the field and lined up to run more plays. However, this time there would be contact. The running back had to take a handoff from the quarterback and try to follow the block of the center and get past two defensive linemen who were lined up on the other side. After taking the handoff, the running back would usually disappear into the maw of the linemen like Jonah into the mouth of the whale, and the collision would be so fierce that you could hear it from the dorms on the other side of campus. It was called the nutcracker drill, and the only good thing about it was that, like a kamikaze mission, you only had to do it once.

When my turn came, I was stiff with fear. I had had a concussion when I was at Fatima as a result of a football accident, and I was sure that this drill was going to send me to the hospital again.

"TWO THIRTY-SEVEN!" the QB shouted. "TWO THIRTY-SEVEN! HUT! HUT!"

I lunged forward and took the ball. Then came the full-body collision—it felt like I had run into a refrigerator. The next thing I knew, I was on my back.

I got to my feet, but I was so dizzy I began walking in the wrong direction—away from the team.

Denny appeared at my side and pulled me around. "You okay, Judgie?" he asked. "You gonna make it?"

"I'm going again."

"What? Are you insane?"

"I'm going again."

The collision had triggered something. I had faced my fear, and now I wanted to prove to Clancy, Carmen, and everyone else that I could take every bit as much—no, more—than they could. It was time to settle my bet.

I went back and stepped into the front of the line.

"Hey, what's the deal?" the guy in the front of the line said.

I ignored him and got into a three-point stance.

The quarterback took the snap. I was clobbered again, but this time I managed to stay on my feet and even struggle through to the other side.

The next morning, when Clancy emerged from the gym door, he added something to his usual "good day to die" greeting. I had caught a punt and was about to toss it back to the kicker when Clancy broke his string of staccato rallying cries and turned to me. "THAT'S THE WAY TO CATCH THAT BALL, MR. JUDGE! YOU KNOW THAT WE DON'T NEED ANY MAVERICKS ON THIS TEAM, MR. JUDGE! ISN'T THAT RIGHT, MR. JUDGE?"

"YES SIR. NO MAVERICKS."

While the others thought Clancy was trying to warn me against goofing off, I knew what he meant: He was talking about me going twice during the nutcrackers. However, his tone of voice was leavened with a hint of humor; he wasn't actually angry, and I imagined he might have even admired me for my guts.

I felt a surge of pride and acceptance. In my entire life, my father had never encouraged me like that about anything.

That next day, we played our first scrimmage against each other. I was put in at defensive back, the defender who covers the wide receiver.

It was a humid and overcast morning, the sky the color of a bruise. Right before we began, there was a loud clap of thunder and it started to rain.

On the first play, the wide receiver lined up close to the tight end. After the snap, I zeroed in on the running back, who I knew was going to get the ball, and rushed into the backfield and collided with him head first. He went down for a loss.

The next play, I did the same thing, with the same result. The rain started to come down harder, the humidity making the inside of my helmet slick with moisture.

The next time we lined up, I noticed a splotch of red on my jersey. I touched my face and my hand came away covered in blood. I had a bloody nose.

I looked up and saw Shane watching me. "You okay?" he asked.

I nodded. In fact, although my head was pounding and blood was running out of my nose like water, I was swept up with exhilaration. In many so-called primitive cultures, part of the ritual of initiating an adolescent male into adulthood is to intentionally "cut" him—in essence, give him a bloody lip. Standing there taking a shower in water and my own blood imbued me with a resolve and an esteem I had never known before. I had faced down my fears and was becoming a member of the tribe. For the first time, my uniform felt like it fit.

At the end of the two weeks, I was so sore I could barely walk. I was also so anxious to get my lips around a beer that I calculated the hours until the O'Neals's party. "Forty-two hours until blast-off," I would say to Shane, checking my watch.

I felt great. I had held my own against the other players and was in the best shape of my life. Even so, I still had doubts that I would make the team. There were too many guys with more experience who had won Clancy's favor long before I appeared. The best I could do, I thought, was to be "optioned." Players who were optioned were given a choice by coach Clancy: they could stay on the team, but they would never play. The option was usually reserved for seniors who wanted to stay with their buddies on the team, but who normally would get cut.

Finally, the last day of camp came. If I was going to be optioned, it was going to happen today. But it no longer mattered to me whether or not I made the team. I had made it. I had survived, even thrived.

I went downstairs and fell in with the other players jammed into the foyer in front of the cafeteria doors, which were still locked. I was standing next to Denny, who was wearing a baseball hat. It was forbidden to wear hats in the cafeteria during the year, but Denny thought that since this was camp it was different.

He was wrong. We were all talking and shoving each other around when an unmistakable voice erupted from the back.

"THERE WILL BE NO HATS WORN IN THIS BUILDING, GENTLEMEN."

It was Father Carmen. But the words were no sooner out of his mouth than Shane, bolstered by his undetectable position deep in the bowels of the throng, rejoined with a dead-on imitation: "IF I SEE A HAT, SAY HELLO TO THE WALL, BECAUSE YOU'RE GOING THROUGH IT." The hall erupted with laughter.

Carmen went nuts. While he hadn't caught exactly what was

said or by whom, he knew that the roar of laughter had resulted from some smart-ass comment made somewhere near the front. And the first person he zeroed in on was me.

Carmen had not seen me say anything, however, and therefore couldn't charge me directly. His only recourse was to try to humiliate me in public. He waited until we had all gotten our food and said grace, then called for order.

"Gentlemen, for the past three years we have had successful camps. There have been no disruptions or disciplinary problems. There has been respect." He paused, eyeing the room. No one moved.

"I would like to make sure that this year is no different. If we are serious about what we want to accomplish, we can't have people disrupting our routine. Is that clear?"

Carmen then turned and looked directly at me. "I WANT TO HEAR IT, MR. JUDGE."

"Yes, Father," I said. Even though I hadn't done a thing, I didn't say anything.

Of course, Clancy had seen the whole thing, and it didn't bode well for the last day of camp, when he doled out the option to players he didn't want on the team.

During calisthenics, the optioning began. I noticed Clancy approach two players and have a long, intense conversation with them. He was giving them the option.

Clancy came down my row, but when he came to me, he just kept walking.

"You made it!" Shane hissed from behind me.

I had. Without being optioned and having never worn a football uniform, I had made the team.

I immediately called home and told my parents the news.

"That's great, Mark," my father said without emotion. "But I want you to make sure you're careful."

His voice was heavy with worry, but there was also something more. For the first time I realized that by going out for the team to win his favor, I might have done the exact wrong thing. He had grown up in the shadow of a famous athlete, and maybe he didn't relish the idea of being the father of one.

I said good-bye and tried to put it out of my mind. After two weeks of sweat, sore muscles, no girls, dirty clothes, and Clancy screaming at us, I could hardly wait to get to the O'Neals's end-of-summer party. I felt like a POW who was about to be released at Mardi Gras. I couldn't wait to see Laura and had even bought rubbers in anticipation that we were going to have sex. Although we hadn't spoken in two weeks, I was sure she was over what had happened at the Four Seasons.

By eleven o'clock, the O'Neals's house and backyard were filled with people, most of whom were drunk. We managed to get away with this under the nose of our parents simply because of the sheer space the O'Neals had in their house. While there was always mingling between the generations at the O'Neals's party, it was the practice that the younger people would have the large patio and pool area to themselves, while the parents kept to the house. This often made it seem as though there were two different parties going on. The parents could be inside, while outside we drank, swam, wrestled with each other, and flirted with girls.

Laura arrived, and I immediately knew that something was wrong. After we said hello, she didn't seem interested in hanging out together and kept disappearing to go off with her friends for long periods of time. When I would go to find her, I always felt as if I was interrupting something and that she was annoyed. At one point she was talking to Mike Fitzgerald, a large, good-looking linebacker, and seemed genuinely irritated that I had joined them. When Mike went off to get another beer, I asked her what was wrong.

"Nothing," she said. "I just don't want to bother you while you're hanging out with Shane and Denny and the other guys."

It was a weak excuse, and she knew it. Yet although it would have been obvious to a monkey that she was giving me the brush-off, I didn't want to face it. Instead of just asking her if she didn't want to see me anymore, I found Shane.

"What's up?" he asked.

"Laura is blowing me off."

We looked over at her. She was talking to Mike again.

"She's hot for Fitzgerald, huh?" Shane said.

"I guess so," I said quietly.

He squeezed my shoulder. "Easy there, big fellah. Don't let it bother you. There will be plenty of others."

He got us a couple of beers and we retreated to the poolside, where Denny's younger brothers were doing flips into the water. The pool had been built lower than the patio, so it was possible to get away from the party there without being out of sight or earshot of everyone.

We sat there and drank, watching the boys launch themselves off the diving board and flip, twist, and corkscrew into the water. By now a crowd had gathered on the patio to watch the boys diving. When one would do something spectacular, the audience erupted with applause. The O'Neals's parties often didn't take off until after midnight, when the last guest would arrive and inebriated people started doing things they would regret in the morning.

Suddenly Denny came racing up, waving something in his hand.

"Have you guys seen this?" he asked.

He shoved it in my face. It was the *Saint,* Prep's school newspaper. The first issue always came out during the last week of summer and was mailed to all the students. It was usually filled with a lot of fluff articles about what teachers and students did over the summer.

This time, however, it was different. "Prep Seniors to Do Community Service," announced the headline.

> Without fail, every year at Prep the same disease sweeps through the ranks of the graduating students. Called "senioritis," its symptoms include laziness, cut classes, and a general inability to concentrate on any- thing academic for more than five minutes.
>
> This year, however, the administration believes it has come up with the cure to final-semester lassitude. This year Prep's seniors will take part in a new com- munity outreach program. Spearheaded by Headmaster Carmen, the program will send seniors to work at needy agencies around Washington on Sundays. The boys will have to keep a journal of their experiences, which will be turned in at the end of the year. The seniors will receive a grade for the journals, and those who fail will not graduate. The project will begin in January and run through the spring.

"Oh my God," I muttered. "There's no way I can get up at six o'clock in the morning on Sunday. I'll die of cottonmouth."

"This is beyond belief," Denny growled. "They can't do this."

"I knew I should have run faster to art class freshman year," Shane said.

"You know why they're doing this, don't you?" Denny said. "They know we go out and get tanked every weekend, and they want to make getting up on Sundays hell."

"We have to do something," I said. "They can't get away with this our senior year."

"What are we going to do?" Shane said, laughing. "Drink a hundred kegs and brag about it?"

No one laughed. For a second, no one even spoke.

"It's brilliant," I said.

"Wait a minute," Shane said. "You can't actually be thinking of—"

"A hundred kegs," I said. "We're going to drink a hundred kegs, then brag about it."

"How?" Shane asked.

Denny crumpled up the *Saint* and tossed it into the pool. "A good first step would be to have our own paper. The *Saint* is nothing but a propaganda machine for Prep."

I sat up. "That's it. We could start our own newspaper. We could drink a hundred kegs, then brag about it in our own paper."

Before I could further the plans for a hundred kegs and our own paper, I was distracted by a loud voice cheering behind us—Laura. She was drunk and kept hooting with encouragement every time one of the kids would hit the water. I turned around a couple of times to see her, but the floodlight attached to the second floor of the house was focused on the pool, and all I could make out were silhouettes. It was like trying to see the audience while on stage.

One of the boys did an elegant reverse swan dive, turning his back to the audience.

"Woooo!" Laura bellowed. "Nice butt!"

"That's it," Shane said, putting his beer down. "She wants a butt, that what she's going to get."

He got up and ducked behind a bush. When he emerged, he was stripped down to his boxer shorts. Then, taking off from twenty feet behind the diving board, he bounded to the edge of the pool, leapt off the side, and launched himself off the diving board.

At the apex of his flight, in one motion, Shane rotated and dropped his shorts to point his ass in the direction of Laura's voice.

Half the crowd went wild. There was a deafening cheer and cries of "9.9! 9.9!"

Unfortunately, half the audience didn't make a sound. While Shane and I had been drinking by the pool, the wall between the parents on the inside and the kids on the outside had been breached. The parents had heard the cheering for the divers and had come outside to watch.

Mr. and Mrs. Cuddy were on Shane in a second. Mr. Cuddy

got about an inch from Shane's face and said something. Shane came over to gather up his clothes, then disappeared into the house. He was done for the night.

I got up, feeling very drunk. I decided I had to find Laura and try to patch things up. I had waded about halfway through the patio when someone stepped in my way.

It was Mary, my old girlfriend. She was drunk.

"I have to tell you something," she said.

"Does it have to be now?" I asked. "I'm looking for someone."

"I know. You're looking for Laura. You dumped me to have sex with her."

"Mary, it's not like that."

"Yes it is," she said. "I really thought we had something special, but you're just like all the other guys. But none of that matters now. I just wanted to let you know that I saw Laura walk off with Mike Fitzgerald, so you might not want to go looking for her."

I looked at her. "She what?"

"She wandered off into the backyard with Fitzgerald. That backyard is the size of my neighborhood, so you might not even find them. If I were you, I would just stay here and get wasted."

I thought that Mary would have enjoyed watching me get burned the way I had burned her, but there was no malice in her face.

"I need a drink," I said. We went to the keg and filled our cups. Then I headed out to the backyard.

"You going back there?" Mary said.

"Yep."

"You want some company?"

"Sure."

We were halfway through the field when I almost tripped over two people. They were rolling around on the ground, making out. The guy had his shirt off. It was Laura and Mike.

"Oh God, Mark," she said. "I'm sorry, I just—"

"Forget it," I said, walking away. "I don't really give a shit."

Mary and I walked to the edge of the field where there was a row of pine trees, and lay down to watch the stars. As we listened to the distant cheers by the pool, I told myself I should just go home. School was about to start, and it would be a good sign if my parents found me in my own bed in the morning.

Still, I didn't move. I wasn't ready to deal with my dad, who hadn't come to the party. He was most likely in his den, drunk, and the twenty feet between his room and mine could be harder to get through than the nutcracker drill.

"I want you to know that I'm sorry about what I did to you," I said to Mary. "And that I know I'm a jerk."

"Yes, you are," she said.

chapter

" I ' m   N o t   a   D r u n k "

I opened one eye and peered at the alarm clock—6:10 A.M. It was the first day of our community project.

This wasn't happening. It was Sunday morning, and the night before we had polished off keg number sixty-two. For the past four months, we had thrown parties every weekend as well as after school, and had even snuck a keg into the parking lot during a basketball game. We were going to be graduating in May, and now that football was over, we had one objective: 100 kegs. The football team had gone five and four, but, more important, we had emptied more than sixty kegs, bringing us within sight of the magic number.

However, the keg count had started to take its toll on me. The night before, Shane and Denny had wisely gone home at midnight, but I had stayed up until three o'clock drinking. I had reached the point where once I had the first beer, I found it impossible to stop until I was completely annihilated. That first, magical cold one seemed to set off a physiological need for more, like a morsel of food offered to a starving man. Once I felt the first lilting rise of a buzz, I had to keep drinking until I could hardly walk. Many of the other guys were the same way; while some got sick after just a few beers, the hard-core drinkers could go all night, and often did. None of us found this disturbing in the least. Our parents drank, our brothers and sisters drank, our aunts and uncles drank—even the Jesuits had a stash of kegs in their living quarters at Prep. To us, being members of what I called "Alcoholics Unanimous" was as natural as a swan drifting into the water.

The main problem, of course, was that I had hangovers that felt as if I had been on the losing side of a battering ram.

After my dad called me, I slid out of bed and hobbled to the shower, then got dressed. When I went downstairs, Shane, Denny, and my father were sitting at the kitchen table.

"It's a beautiful morning," my dad said, smiling. "The birds have been up since five."

My dad loved the early morning. No matter how much he had had to drink the night before, he was always up early, watching the birds and squirrels cavorting in the backyard.

I grunted, pouring a soda down my throat.

"Is that all you're going to have for breakfast?" my dad asked.

"I'll eat at the shelter."

"Jesus, you look like roadkill," Shane said when we got into his car. "How late did you stay last night?"

I held up three fingers.

Denny winced. "That's got to hurt."

I stretched out in the backseat. Shane pulled around a corner, and my stomach turned.

"Oh shit," I moaned.

Denny glanced back. "You gonna get sick?"

"I'll make it," I said. I started breathing through my nose and out through my mouth, a trick I had learned to settle the stomach.

"Remember," Denny said, "we're meeting at my house tonight to put together our new paper."

I shut my eyes. Football season had kept us too busy to launch our underground paper, but tonight we would get started. I had collected photos and art supplies from the yearbook office, and Denny had a desktop publishing program on his computer.

For our community service job, Shane, Denny, and I were assigned to a soup kitchen in one of the poorest parts of DC. It was off New York Avenue, a drug-infested neighborhood of broken-down row houses and empty lots. The building was a two-story row house in the middle of a block whose only other life was the corner liquor store. Downstairs was the kitchen, upstairs the cafeteria. Our job was to pick up leftover rolls donated from a local supermarket, stir soup, make sandwiches, and generally be around if we were needed for anything.

When I came through the doors of the soup kitchen that first morning, I was more toxic than any other addict in the place. Although it was freezing, I was sweating, and the smell of bean soup almost made me retch.

Inside, we were met by a thin, older black woman named Ruth. She was a social worker who helped run the kitchen. She took our coats and put us to work making sandwiches and stirring the soup.

For the first hour, I managed to stay on my feet. I still felt sick, but avoided food service by volunteering for some sweeping and clean-up work. The place was about half full with people I could only guess were homeless. A couple of them were almost invisible under their layers of clothing, and some talked to themselves. Others just looked tired or bored, and sat around talking and smoking cigarettes.

I was starting on the kitchen when the front door blew open. Directly in front of me was a tall black man. He was wearing a Redskins cap and was wrapped in so many layers of clothing, all that was showing were his eyes.

He looked right at me. He began to snap his fingers and hum. It sounded like swing music.

Ruth, who was helping Denny clean a pan, glanced over. "Hey, honey," she said.

"I'll be jumpin' the blues until the day I die," he sang again. He peeled his coat and hat off and put them on a chair. He was in his late thirties and was clean cut, with a button-down white dress shirt and brown corduroy slacks.

"Hey, Mom, I got a new move," he said to Ruth.

"Let's have it, Ronnie," Ruth said.

He jumped over to Ruth, and they suddenly started dancing.

It was unlike anything I had ever seen, except maybe in an old movie. It was swing, but not like the swing I saw my parents doing at weddings. It was more complicated yet more graceful and energetic, with more kicks, turns, and flips, and theatrical hesitations.

"Damn, what is that?" Denny asked.

"It's the Lindy Hop," Ruth said, ducking under Ronnie's arm for a turn. "It's the dance that swing came out of. It's actually a lot more complicated than swing, as you can tell. I taught Ronnie when he was a little boy, after I had learned it from Frankie Manning in 1942. Frankie was the greatest Lindy Hopper of all time. He used to dance with Duke Ellington's band."

They danced for a few more seconds; then, with an arm-waving flourish, Ronnie lowered his mother into a dip. Everyone in the kitchen began to applaud, and Ronnie wheeled around and faced me.

"You know how to swing dance?" he asked.

"Uh, 'fraid not."

"Oh, *man,*" he said. "*Everyone* should know how to swing."

"I didn't know people did that anymore."

"Well sure they do. Down at Glen Echo, near the river in Maryland. There's an old ballroom down there—the Spanish Ballroom. They swing down there."

I had heard of it. Glen Echo was just a few miles from my

house. It had been an amusement park until it closed in the 1960s, but they still held swing dances there.

Before I could object, he had grabbed me and spun me around. "Just follow my lead," he said. "I'll do the hard part."

I should have stopped him, but it was too late. Between the bender from the night before and the putrid stench of five-bean soup, I couldn't keep it down.

I tumbled outside, then slipped into the alley next to the building. I barely made it to the trash can when I started getting sick.

Ronnie came up behind me and began softly patting me on the back. "Sorry, man," he said. "I didn't know you were so hungover."

"I'm all right," I gasped and spat. "I just have the flu or something." I turned to retch again.

"Just take it easy," he said. "I've been there. That rotgut will get you every time."

I finished and turned around. Ronnie was standing behind me.

"I have to go home," I said.

"You had too much last night," he said.

"I did not," I said, irritated. "I told you, I'm sick."

He shook his head and chuckled. "You can't fool me, man. You can't fool another drunk."

I glared at him. I pushed myself off the wall and started

walking back. I felt dizzy, then stumbled and fell into a pile of trash.

"Easy there," Ronnie said. He helped me to a clean spot, then knelt down and patted my shoulder.

"Just relax," he said. "Take a deep breath."

I closed my eyes and tried to breathe slowly.

"Alcohol," Ronnie said, sadly shaking his head. "It's a killer."

"I'm not a drunk," I said.

"Uh-huh. That's what I said until it ruined my life. I should have been a doctor."

I looked at him incredulously.

"Yeah, I know it's hard to believe *now*, but I was in med school a few years ago, at Howard. I was going to be a pathologist—study disease in cells and tissues. I've loved science since I was in high school over at Wilson. You know Wilson—we play Prep in football. My grades were so good I got a scholarship to Howard. I started drinking the first week of my freshman year, and by the end of my second year, I was out.

"For the next five years, I drank. I lived with my mother, so I had a place to stay. But I couldn't hold down a job. Then one day, I was in an alley behind a liquor store going through a trash can for booze. The store owner would sometimes throw away the defective bottles without pouring out the booze, and I would fetch them out.

"I was in the dumpster, near the bottom, when I just

stopped. It was like I had been possessed or something. I just stood there, buried so deep in the trash it was dark, and I had what alcoholics call 'a moment of clarity.' It struck me that if I kept going the way I was, I was going to die like that, stranded in a dumpster. Right then and there I got on my knees, and said, 'God, I can no longer control myself. I need your help.' After a few minutes like that, just praying, I got out. I was a new man. I went to my first AA meeting that night, and the next time I tried to get drunk, I couldn't. Straight up, man. I had prayed for God to remove the addiction, and He did just that. After that first AA meeting, I bought a pint and drank it straight down, but nothing happened. I didn't get drunk. That told me the party was over. I've been sober for a year."

Listening to Ronnie, I realized that somewhere between my first drink with Seamus on the beach and my last from the keg the night before, I had lost my faith. Ronnie was talking about God in a way that was completely alien to me. It was as if he knew God personally and had complete faith in Him. All my belief, my rapture at the Stations of the Cross, all those hours I would stare into the face of Jesus on the cross and feel his boundless love for me, were gone.

I sat there blinking into the cold early-morning sun, stunned. I no longer cared about my faith. I was not yet hostile to the very idea of religion, but it had never imbued me with the kind of mystical bliss that came out of the tap at O'Rourke's. My god was now alcohol.

"Here," Ronnie said, handing me a scrap of paper with his name and number on it. "Put that in your wallet. You might need it someday."

That night, Shane, Denny and I got together in Denny's basement to put together the paper.

We decided to call it the *Heretic.* Our main objectives for the paper—which was nothing more than a few photocopied pages of articles and clumsy art collages—were twofold: to insult people and to report on what the *Saint,* the official school paper, ignored: who had what party, who had embarrassed themselves, who had the worst haircuts on campus, who was getting laid, and, most important, how much we were drinking. The *Heretic* was the official journal of the 100-keg quest and everything that happened on the way.

We parodied the *Saint,* stealing section headings—Student Spotlight, Social Beat—and wrote articles that in any other paper would have landed us in jail for libel. Our dance and dating column, "Social Beat," was about "when the news really hit the ceiling"—an obvious reference to masturbation. In "Faculty Spotlight," we celebrated the most embarrassing or idiosyncratic characteristic of a particular teacher. For our profile of Father

Hartsby, the young priest who was into punk rock, we cut-and-pasted his hair so it looked like a mohawk.

We also championed whoever was behind a rash of vandalism directed at the houses of Catholic girls. Several girls from Stone Ridge, Holy Child, Visitation, and other all-girls Catholic schools had gone on vacation with their parents only to come back and find their houses covered in toilet paper and shaving cream. The culprits had never been caught. Some homes were so completely draped with toilet paper and shaving cream that you couldn't see a blade of grass or a window pane. There had only been one witness, an old woman nobody believed who claimed that one of the perpetrators was a priest.

We finished the paper at eleven. By the time I got home it was after midnight, and when I pulled into the driveway my heart sank.

My father was up. I could see him sitting at his desk reading, a tall drink at his elbow.

I braced myself for another confrontation. It was after midnight on a school night, and he would probably be drunk and spoiling for a fight.

His den was the first room in the house, so there was no sneaking past. As soon as I pushed the front door open, he jumped, then wheeled around in his chair and looked at his watch.

"It's twelve-thirty," he said with exaggerated shock. "Where have you been?"

"I was out with Shane and Denny."

He stood up. "You're still in high school, Mark. You guys can't be out all hours every night."

I reached into my backpack and handed him a copy of the *Heretic*. "We were working on this," I said.

He took the paper, then slowly walked back into his den and sat down. He took a sip from his drink, placed the paper in front of him, and began to read. I stood there, afraid to move.

About a minute later it happened. His shoulders started to shake, then his whole body.

He was laughing.

"Hey, this is pretty good stuff," he said.

I came into the den and looked over his shoulder. He was looking at the fake "wanted" poster we had created of Corey Joyce, Prep's biggest troublemaker and the kid who had fallen through my parent's ceiling at my party. Recently, Corey had been busted for driving while intoxicated. The police had found bishop's vestments in the backseat of his car, including a hat and staff, which Joyce had explained by claiming that he was on his way home from a costume party.

To report the story in the *Heretic,* we had cut out a picture of the pope and superimposed prison bars over him. "Wanted," the headline read, "for Driving While Intoxicated, Resisting Arrest, and Vatican II."

When we distributed the copies the next day, it caused a sensation. We made a hundred copies and handed them out in the morning, and by lunch you couldn't walk into the cafeteria or library without seeing someone either doubled over laughing or with his head deep in its pages. This included some teachers, many of whom could be seen surreptitiously reading an issue in the bathroom and laughing to themselves.

Still, we didn't know what to expect. We hadn't heard from Carmen, and although the paper was anonymous, it wouldn't be hard to trace us to it.

By the final period, he knew. I was hustling out of Shakespeare when I almost ran into him.

He pulled me aside.

"One false move, and you guys are *out,*" he hissed. "One tasteless joke, one vulgar quip, one ribald jest, and you and O'Neal and Cuddy are spending the rest of your final semester with your parents. Understand?"

I nodded.

"One more thing. There's been an outbreak of vandalism directed against the homes of Catholic girls around Washington. I want to know who's behind it."

"I have no idea," I stammered. It was the truth.

He watched me closely for a few seconds, then marched back to his office.

● ● ● ● ●

For the next few months, everything was cool. We put the paper out every two weeks. We panned the school plays, complained about the food, reprinted huge tabs from O'Rourke's, kept tabs on the keg count—which by March was into the mid-eighties—and griped about having to get up and go to our community service, dropping hints that none of us were keeping our journals. While most guys were just lazy and wanted to wait until the last minute, I found the whole idea of keeping a journal insulting to Ronnie, Ruth, and the others at the shelter. It was as if we were anthropologists on an expedition and were required to report all of our deep and profound sorrow at the plight of these poor people. I felt as if, in a way, we were using them for a grade.

Finally, spring came. We began to get more excited about graduating.

It was around this time that the *Heretic* came across a real scoop: I finally discovered who was behind the crime spree. I found out because the perpetrator found me. I was in the bathroom between classes when Corey Joyce came in and lit a cigarette—an offense that meant instant suspension from Prep.

"You better put that out, Joyce," I said. "If Carmen comes in here, you're history."

He stepped into the stall next to me. "Shut up and listen," he whispered. "I only have a few minutes. There's something that the *Heretic* should know about. I'm going to say it all quickly, so listen close."

I had finished going to the bathroom, but I just stood there.

"I'm the one doing those houses," he said. "A few months back I formed a group of highly trained assault troops. We dress up like priests, brothers, and bishops, and go do a girl's house. We only do students from Washington's finer virgin vaults and only strike when she and her family are away."

"Oh my God," I muttered.

"Yes sir," he said smugly, then took a drag. "We call ourselves the Inquisitors."

I zipped up, then pulled a pad out of my backpack. "Let me get some of this down."

He stepped back from the stall and held his hands up. "Whoa there, stud. Let's just take this one step at a time. The only reason I'm telling you is that for the last four months we've been so good at our job that there's a chance I could graduate without anyone knowing I'm behind it. I don't want to get busted and not graduate, but I do want the world to know what I've done. If you do it, you can't publish the issue until after we graduate."

"Deal," I said.

"We're only going to do one more job," he said, "and I want a massive turnout—at least fifty guys. We've been working small, in groups of ten or twelve, but I want to go out with a bang. Especially since we're doing Barbara Gordon's house."

I almost dropped my pen. Barbara Gordon was the daughter of a senator who was one of the most conservative men in United States politics. She went to St. Catherine's and lived in a mansion in Potomac, about five miles from my parents' house. Her house was the size of a hotel.

"It's going to be the Sistine Chapel of rolling," Corey said.

I didn't know what to say. I had gone out with Barbara a couple of times, and she was a very bright, funny, and nice person. She was also a close friend of Becky, my next-door neighbor and Shane's girlfriend.

"Why Barbara?" I asked. "She's cool."

He shrugged. "There's no rhyme or reason to it," he said. "We put a bunch of names in a hat, and whoever comes out gets it. We're equal opportunity."

"When is this going down?" I said.

"Next Saturday night. The Gordons are going to be in Texas for the weekend. We'll meet at my house at ten o'clock. My folks are away."

"What about costumes?"

He pulled a card out of his wallet. "There's a store in Wheaton that sells religious uniforms," he said. "It's our supplier."

He checked his watch, then stamped out the cigarette. "I gotta go. I'm meeting with some of the boys in five minutes."

"One more thing," I said. "Why?"

He thought for a second. "Because they're there."

Actually, there was more to it. When I checked the list of girls who had been hit, I noticed that all of them were, like Barbara, friends with guys who went to Prep—including, in a couple of cases, Corey himself. There was no escaping how provincial the Catholic community was. In the four years of high school, a lot of these girls had become like sisters to us, and that was exactly the impetus for the attacks: in the classic little-brother syndrome, we were doing it just for the simple joy of pestering our sisters.

That night Shane, Denny, and I put together the latest issue of the *Heretic*. Along with the usual idiocy, we ran a small, arch notice:

This Saturday there will be a senior hayride. It begins at Corey Joyce's house at 10:00 P.M. and goes until midnight. All seniors are invited.

A few days later, Shane, Denny, and I arrived at Corey's house exactly at ten.

When we came through the door, it was like stepping into a Vatican convention. I was surrounded by about thirty guys dressed as Catholic clergy. There were priests, bishops, brothers, monks—even a couple of nuns. Corey had gone all out for the occasion, again renting a full bishop's outfit. He had a miter—the pointy hat that bishops wear—an avocado green vestment that went down to his toes, and a staff. He looked like a parody of the Pope.

"Keg's in the corner, boys," he said. "You might want to get lubricated before this."

I was on the keg in a second. I drank down three beers, one right after the other. There was no way I was going to do this sober. Contrary to the cliché that drunks drink because they're depressed, I often drank to heighten my joy and excitement.

I was on my third beer when Corey held up his hands and called for quiet.

"My brothers and sisters," he said, nodding toward the nuns. "We are gathered here this evening for a very special reason—to destroy a young woman's home."

A few cheers went up, but most of us were laughing. Joyce was playing his part of high priest to the hilt.

"The land is defiled with the scourge of sin," he hollered, raising a fist in the air. "It is the sin of arrogance, and the guilty are rich Catholic schoolgirls. Under the lash of their tyranny, we are forced into a compromise with Satan. We are forced to endure inane chatter with their fathers before taking them out. They make us obey their curfews. They must repent and be punished!"

A cheer went up.

Corey looked at his watch. "Fellow soldiers of God, it is now midnight. Let the Inquisition ride!"

We piled into our cars. I had driven myself because Barbara lived near my house in Potomac, and if there was trouble, I could easily escape home.

The Gordon's house was in west Potomac, in land that was still used for horse farming, and as we got closer the well-lit sub-urban streets became dark and curvy country roads.

When we got to the Gordons' neighborhood, however, we immediately ran into problems. The house was like a well-guarded fortress. It stood on the top of a hill in the middle of the woods and was only accessible through a dark and narrow driveway. It had rained recently, and the ditches on either side of the driveway were too muddy to walk through. We drove around back, but that part was surrounded by a thirty-foot-high hedge. If we got caught rolling the house, it would be impossible to escape without being caught.

On top of all that, the family was home. There were lights on inside and cars in the driveway. After Corey snuck up to investigate, he came back shaking his head.

"We're screwed," he said. "We got bad information. Either they canceled their trip or it's next week."

We pulled into an adjacent neighborhood so as not to be seen.

Corey leapt onto the hood of his car, dragging his vestments behind him.

"Listen up!" he called, and we gathered around him. "While the Inquisitors fear nothing, discretion is the better part of valor. Perhaps we should roll the Gordons on another night. *Res Ipsa Loquitur.*"

"Wimp!" someone shouted from the back. One of the nuns belched.

He lifted his hands to silence the crowd. "Gentlemen, gentlemen. A house divided cannot stand. We need to consider our options and—"

He stopped talking. He was now looking above our heads, at something in the distance.

"Oh, shit," he muttered.

We all turned around as one, just in time to see the police car heading toward us.

"Fall back!" Corey shouted, leaping off the hood and into his car.

I jumped into my car and started to speed away. I glanced in the rearview mirror and saw the cop behind me. His red and blue lights flashed on. He was gaining on me.

Corey's car was in front of me. We were on a long empty

stretch of country road, but I knew the area and remembered that there was a farm coming up around the bend. It had a long driveway, and if I pulled into it and killed my lights, the cops might miss me.

We rounded the corner, and the mailbox appeared on the left. I turned into the driveway so hard the car almost flipped. I hit the lights and sped to the top.

I sat there in the darkness, listening to myself breathe and peering into the rearview mirror.

The flashing blue and red lights appeared on the road. They passed the driveway, then, about halfway down the hill, came to a stop.

It had to be Corey. He had been right in front of me.

I slowly backed down the driveway. I glanced just long enough to see Corey stopped in front of the police car. I turned the other way and was gone.

By Monday morning, news was all over Prep that Corey had been arrested. At first, however, none of us were worried. "I didn't tell the cops squat," Corey said to me during Latin class. "Luckily, I hadn't had too much to drink, so I passed the Breathalyzer test. He didn't even check my car. He didn't even tie me to any of the other raids. To him, we were just a bunch of dumb kids going for a joyride."

By the time lunch came around, everyone was sure that the whole thing would blow over, and we were even making plans to go back and do the Gordons right. We were on our dessert when Father Carmen came into the hall and called for our attention.

"Gentlemen," he said. "It is now May, and in a couple of short weeks you will graduate. For five months you have been doing your community service jobs and keeping a journal about your experiences. As you know, those journals were scheduled to be due at the end of the month, right before graduation. However, certain events have recently taken place that make it necessary to see them as soon as possible. You are to bring them in tomorrow."

The reaction in the room was so intense yet controlled it was comical. None of us had even started our journals. We were seniors in our last semester, and every assignment we were given was being done at the last possible minute.

Someone even protested. "But Father," he squeaked, "they're not supposed to be due until the end of May."

"That was indeed once the case," Carmen snapped back, "but recent events have given Loyola Prep a black eye, and I want to make sure that I can inform parents that their sons are working and not driving around drinking and vandalizing houses."

The room went dead.

"I'm sure you're wondering how I figured this out," he said. "Just let me say that I can imagine you guys doing just about anything *except* having a hayride. And if Mr. Joyce has been working alone, he must have ten arms."

He had figured it out. We had given the game away by putting that dumb, obvious notice in the *Heretic* about the hayride. Carmen had seen it, figured out that something was up, and tipped off the cops. Now he was going to make sure that none of us graduated on time.

That night, we were up all night trying to compose our diaries, pacing the floor and trying to remember the day-to-day experiences of our community service. I wrote until my hand was too cramped to open. In the end, most of the journal consisted of conversations, half imaginary and half real, that I had had with Ronnie about his life and alcoholism. Anything to fill pages. I didn't include anything he had said about my own drinking, of course.

Two days later, Father Carmen's voice came over the intercom. "The following students report to my office immediately," he said. Then he read off a list of twenty names, including Shane, Denny, and me.

When we got down to Carmen's office, there was a line of guys waiting to get in.

"We're screwed," Denny whispered.

My turn came. Father Carmen was sitting behind his desk, reading something.

"Sit down," he said without looking up.

I sat. Finally he looked at me. "Ah yes," he said. "Mr. Judge."

I smiled, feeling like an idiot.

He leaned back in his chair and bit on the top of a pen.

"You finished your journal?" he said.

"I just handed it in," I replied. My voice was quavering. I was using every ounce of energy to sound innocent, failing miserably.

"Uh-huh," he said. "Let me ask you this. How long did it take you to do it?"

I shrugged, trying to appear confused at this bizarre line of questioning. "It took me, you know, about five months."

"Uh-huh." He reached over to his desk and pulled up the journal I had submitted. He started leafing through it, stopping at various places to read. "It seems like you and this Ronnie character have quite a friendship."

"Yes, Father."

"So, if I called him, he could vouch for everything that's in here?"

I felt heat rise into my face like helium into a balloon.

"Uh, I don't know. He has a bad memory, you know. He drinks a lot. There's been some long-term damage, you know, to his memory."

"Uh-huh," he said.

He set down the journal and let out a sigh. "Okay, Mr. Judge, here's the deal. I don't think you took this assignment seriously, and I'm going to fail you. You'll have to take a class at a community college this summer before you get your diploma. I also think you should spend graduation day doing your community service."

For some reason, suddenly I didn't care what Carmen did. I felt as if I had been bullied and was ready to fight back. We had all put four years and thousands of dollars into Prep, and because of one stupid diary they weren't going to let us graduate on time. Sure, my parents were going to go nuts. But I could tell just by looking at Carmen that this was a foregone conclusion—they had already decided not to let us graduate, and all of this was just a little bit of torture for their pleasure. I wasn't going to give him the satisfaction.

I shrugged. "I guess you'll just have to do what you think is right."

He looked startled. "You mean you don't care about this?" Carmen said.

"I get the idea that whatever is going to happen is out of my hands, and nothing I can say right now will change it."

"Fine," Carmen said. "We'll be contacting your parents tomorrow. That gives you tonight to break the news to them if you want."

For a second, I almost said something. I could take not graduating on time—I had been through worse. But what I couldn't take was being herded into the dean's office and lined up like bowling pins, then given the impression that there was something we could do or say to reverse what had happened. We had been caught red-handed, and they should have just said so. *Tell this jerk off,* I said to myself. *Go out with a bang.*

"Good day, Mr. Judge."

That evening, right when my father got home, I gave him and my mother the news. I wanted to do it before my father had a chance to have his first drink. When he was sober, he took bad news much better. Indeed, one of my parents' biggest strengths was their defensiveness of the family which always prevented them from holding a grudge or staying mad at us long. When my parents got bad news, they didn't holler or beat us—the incident with my brother getting caught selling dope was the exception that proved the rule—they imploded with disappointment. Then, sometimes in record time, they rebounded, dealt with the problem, and forgot about it.

However, this was on a scale that they weren't used to. Compared with me, my siblings were ready for canonization. Straight-A student Joe, who had married the doctor, was living in Virginia Beach as the youngest museum curator in the country.

Mike, a big drinker who loved a good time, had launched a successful acting career in Washington. Alyson had graduated from college and was running her own consulting business. The other three had been good students and rarely got into any kind of trouble. While we were far from perfect, we had all come up pretty well.

Until now. When I broke the news to my parents, my father silently made a drink and retreated into his den. He was so upset he didn't even want to look at me. My mother sat in the living room watching TV, too stunned and upset to speak. They were both in shock. They had spent thousands of dollars to give me the best education in the world, and all they wanted in return was to see me accept a piece of paper from Carmen. I had denied them that simple pleasure, and they wouldn't get another chance.

I retreated to my room, and put on a Eurythmics record. The cool, ethereal music reminded me of better times—Beach Week, meeting Mary, hording around with Shane.

The next morning, my parents began to rebound. Other parents whose sons were not graduating—in the final tally there were about twelve of us—were calling to compare notes with my parents. When my parents found out how many had gotten busted, they eased up considerably. My father actually thought that Carmen was out of line. "It was a dumb assignment," he said. "I think it was great to make you guys do service work, but to make high school seniors keep a journal and expect that they would have it done early—that's just crazy."

My mother agreed. She was soon laughing about how "the twelve disciples" had blown graduation and how ridiculous the assignment had been in the first place. By the end of the day, she was almost convinced that Carmen had simply been out to get us.

For my part, I went to the local community college to sign up for a summer course—film appreciation. I would watch movies for six weeks and write about it. This could actually wind up being fun.

However, there was still one piece of unfinished business. The keg count was at ninety-eight. Despite all the trouble we were in, we couldn't end the year without reaching the magic number.

The Saturday night before graduation, a large group of us met in the empty parking lot of the National Cathedral in Washington. The Cathedral is one of the most spectacular churches in DC. Modeled after Notre Dame in Paris, its gray gothic towers reach toward heaven and take up a block the size of a football field. It has a large, dark parking lot in the back, and we had rented a van and put the two kegs in the back.

At the top of the parking lot was a grassy hill with a large Celtic cross in the center. From there you had a panoramic view of the glittering lights of Capitol Hill. Shane, Denny, and I sat at the base of the cross, enjoying the view and getting drunk. Sitting there with my pals, I felt a surge of hope. Sure, I had screwed up badly by not graduating, but I would eventually, and in a few months I was going to college. I had been accepted at Catholic University, which was just a few miles away. Denny had decided to put off school for a year, and we had decided to get an apartment together in Georgetown. I would straighten out, get good grades. Things would be different.

The next day, graduation day, Denny, Shane, and I went to the soup kitchen to work. It was a warm, sunny spring day, and the shelter was only about half full. Ronnie was there with his mother.

"Hey guys," he called to us. "Come over here, my mom can show you how to dance."

"Not now, Ronnie," Shane said, and sat down.

"What's with him?" Ronnie said.

I told him what had happened. He laughed and shook his head.

"Well, it's not the end of the world. I mean, maybe it will teach you a lesson."

"And what would that be?"

"You get more girls if you don't roll their houses." He started snapping his fingers and tapping his foot. "That, and if you know how to dance."

chapter

Disappearing from Life

DENNY AND I RENTED AN APARTMENT IN GEORGETOWN ON 32ND Street, about four blocks from O'Rourke's. My parents agreed to pay my rent as long as I was in school, and I soon settled into a life of getting up, going to class, then going to O'Rourke's to get drunk.

Although my drinking behavior was fairly evident to my family and friends, it didn't set off alarms for anyone for many years. In the past ten years, alcohol has become more of a social taboo in many circles, but when I was growing up, having a daily martini was practically a fashion statement. Even today, when drinking seems to be declining in social acceptance, most people still view alcohol addiction as different from other drug addictions. They readily accept that the use of cocaine, heroin, and even marijuana causes profound and long-term physiological changes in the brain and the body, from jitters and psychotic behavior to cravings and withdrawal, that makes the user addicted. But with alcohol, they assume that psychology is the primary cause of the illness. It doesn't often occur to them that alcoholics might have a genetic and biochemical susceptibility to alcohol that makes the drug as addictive, if not more, than heroin, cocaine, or pot, and that the emotional eruptions that keep surfacing are the result, not the cause, of the chemical ravages of the addiction.

In the book *Seven Weeks to Sobriety: The Proven Program to Fight Alcoholism Through Nutrition,* alcoholism expert Joan

Mathews Larson cites mountains of evidence that point to a specific biochemistry that reacts differently to alcohol. Among the differences are the ability to tolerate huge amounts of alcohol coupled with the inability of the liver to process toxic by-products of the drug. After they build up, toxins get into the bloodstream and brain, where, according to Larson, they form psychoactive compounds that "are remarkably similar to opiates." In short, Larson is claiming that, in intensity, an alcoholic high is not unlike a heroin high.

By this time, I was beginning to suspect that alcohol was affecting me differently than other people. From ancient times to the present, alcoholics have described intoxication in religious language, and I knew why: When I drank, I could feel myself enter a state of religious-like rapture. I would sometimes stay up all night drinking in O'Rourke's, sitting on one of the large windowsills watching the late-night traffic drift by. I was ensconced in a womb of contentment—warm, romantic, completely in the present moment without concern for the past or future.

However, what addiction builds up, it eventually breaks down. For years I did little else but drink, and slowly my brain and body deteriorated. Where once I would experience hours of euphoria from drinking, the length of my ecstasy shrank, the vacuum of a blackout or the jitters of a hangover outweighing the pleasure of intoxication. I would feel exuberant, funny, and charming for a brief time, then lapse into a stupor of moroseness and self-pity, a dark, antisocial version of myself. I was like Gollum, a character in *The Lord of the Rings*. Gollum once resembled a normal, hobbitlike creature, but years of carrying the ring had warped him to the point where he was a sniffling, vicious monster. Indeed, *The Lord of the Rings* itself could be read as a metaphor for the chemical changes brought on by drug addiction. While the magic ring allowed its wearer to disappear, the way alcohol was letting me disappear from life, it had a horrible repercussion: slow physical, mental, and spiritual destitution.

The change took place over the course of several years and was so gradual that Denny, who, as a bartender at O'Rourke's, was my main supplier, didn't even notice. I simply did less reading, studying, going to movies, visiting family, dating, and more and more drinking. I broke the records for consecutive nights spent at O'Rourke's—156. Denny estimated that he had given me three thousand dollars' worth of free drinks, yet he didn't think there was anything wrong. After all, I was in college, and everyone drank a lot in college. Moreover, drinking was part of the culture we had grown up in, and you had to be near death before anyone thought you had a problem. Yet even with the herculean intake of many Irish Catholics, my behavior eventually became so out of control that it gained notice.

It first became obvious over Christmas break of my fourth

year. All the guys planned to meet at O'Rourke's. I went down in the afternoon, and by the time Shane arrived, I was well into my self-pity phase.

"You hear the news?" he asked, shifting into the stool beside me. "Your girlfriend's getting married."

I looked at him. "What?"

"Mary. She's engaged. She met some guy at Boston College."

While the real me had only feelings of friendship for Mary, the alcoholic me saw this as the most egregious betrayal imaginable. *She had run off to college and was making a life for herself, leaving me here to rot in O'Rourke's.*

"Where'd you hear that?" I said.

"She called me earlier. She's home for Christmas and needed your new number. She's probably trying to get in touch with you right now."

I went to the pay phone in the back of the bar and called her.

"Mary?"

"Mark? God, I've been trying to get in touch with you all afternoon. I have some news—"

"I heard. Jesus, Mary, what are you trying to do to me?"

"What?"

"I thought *we* were going to get married."

"Wait a minute. You're drunk. Are you at O'Rourke's?"

"It doesn't matter where I am. Listen, you have to dump this guy."

"What? Are you insane?"

"Mary, listen to me. You must dump this guy. I want to get married."

"Jesus, you're in bad shape, I can tell. Go jump in a cab and go home and crash. Are any of the guys there?"

"Screw the guys. I'm serious. I'm asking you to marry me."

"Mark, go home. You're drunk. We'll talk later."

"Goddammit you bitch, fuck you and your fucking husband. You're not even listening to me."

There was a long silence on the other end. Even as I swayed back and forth, clutching the phone wire for support in a fog of inebriation, I knew I had said a horrible thing. Yet I didn't apologize. It was as though there was a different version of myself—Mr. Hyde—who had taken over my body, and I couldn't stop him.

"Mark," she finally said. "If you keep this up, you're going to have to see Father Paul."

"Father Paul? You mean from Our Lady of Fatima? How do you know him?"

"Because he counsels alcoholics, and my cousin is an alcoholic."

"Wait a minute. Are you saying you think I'm some kind of a drunk?"

"Judging by the way you're acting now, yes. You're acting very strange. I think—"

"I'll tell you what," I said. "I'll go to see Father Paul if you come down here and marry me right now."

"Mark, you'd better go home. Have one of the guys bring you home."

"I hate you," I hissed. "You left me. I hope you get divorced."

"Mark, let me talk to one of the guys. Just hand the phone over. Is Denny bartending?"

I hung up and went back to my bar stool.

"I couldn't help but overhear," Shane said. "I didn't know you cared that much. I wouldn't have told you."

"I have to get out of here," I said.

"Where are you going?" Shane asked.

"Just for a walk. I'll be back in an hour."

I went outside and walked up M street. It was Friday night and the streets were crowded with partiers. I turned right up Wisconsin and found myself in the middle of a scene that wasn't uncommon in Georgetown on a weekend night: the police had arrested a couple of rowdy drunks and were putting them into a paddy wagon. As I walked past, one of the guys struggled free and almost knocked me over trying to get away. Without thinking, I grabbed him.

"Nice catch," the cop said to me, pulling him away.

"Piss off," I snapped. "Why don't you Nazi bastards leave them alone?"

He stopped, then raised a finger and pointed it at me. "One more word out of you and you're going in with them."

"Eat my shorts."

He didn't even blink, just put an iron grip on my arm and wheeled me around. "You have the right to remain silent."

I started to fight him, but another cop pushed me to the ground. I shouted obscenities and spat on their shoes.

They cuffed me, then tossed me in the paddy wagon. The other two guys were in a cruiser.

Taking me to the station, the cops decided to have a little fun. Whenever they would come to a stop sign, they would jam on the brakes so hard that I would go flying ass over elbow, like a tennis shoe in a dryer. Whenever I got back to a sitting position, it was only long enough to see the cop who was driving laughing.

Even though I had been busted, I wasn't too concerned. For one, I was drunk. And growing up with the Prep boys, I had grown accustomed to dealing with cops, whether they were trying to bust up a loud keg party or were kicking us off the beach. Most of my friends had been hauled in at one time or another.

They brought me to the station and charged me with being drunk and disorderly—a $25 fine.

I had exactly $23.68 on me.

The cops must have known that we were suburban punks who would get eaten alive in the holding pen, so instead of putting us in with the other criminals, they allowed us to call for someone to pick us up. I immediately called O'Rourke's, but Shane had left and Denny couldn't just leave the bar to pick me up. It was after midnight, and I couldn't just call any of the other guys—most were home visiting their families, and I couldn't risk waking up their parents.

Finally, when I realized that unless someone arrived with the extra $1.32, I would have to spend the night in a DC jail, I called home. My dad answered.

"Uh, Dad, it's Mark. Um, listen, I've been arrested."

"What?"

"Yeah, I was in Georgetown and I called this cop a Nazi."

"Jesus, Mark, you know better than that. Where are you?"

I gave him the address.

"I'll be right there."

I thought I was dead.

About an hour later he came in, looking as if he had just woken up. He didn't say anything, just paid the fine and led me out to the car.

I expected him to be positively stiff with anger, but the first thing he asked me was if I was all right. My father might have been reluctant to show a lot of emotion and been mean when he drank, but he knew when someone was too dog-tired to need a lecture.

"You look like hell," he said. "Did they beat you up?"

"Not with their hands," I said. "They used the paddy wagon instead."

"You should go home and take it easy for a couple of days. You and the Prep guys always go nuts over Christmas, and this might be a good year to cool it down a bit."

"Maybe you're right. I feel like the hobbits after they were captured by the Orcs." I was referring to a scene in *The Lord of the Rings* where the hobbits are captured by large, apelike creatures called Orcs and forced to march for miles.

Dad smiles. "You know," he said. "I got hauled in once when I was about your age."

"Really?"

"Yeah. Me and some of the Fitzgerald boys. For stealing hubcaps. It was in Chevy Chase. Back in those days, the cops knew all our parents. It was a different world."

When I got home, it was almost two. I thought about calling Mary. Then I decided against it. The truth was, I didn't care about her getting married. I had just been drunk when I heard the news. It could have been anything that set me off. The chemical had created a monster, and in the state I was in, I was going to run over anything that got in my way.

.   I found a bottle of tequila that Denny had tried to hide in the freezer and sat in the kitchen in the dark, drinking. I felt confused about my dad. He should have gone through the roof over this one, but he hadn't. In a way, it made me feel worse. If anyone had an ass-kicking coming, it was me. I realized that I was luckier than most kids, whose fathers beat them or never read books or didn't care about anything but football. Maybe this could be the start of a new understanding between me and my father, I thought. Maybe I was starting to grow up and could let him be himself, without expecting the world or resenting it when he didn't give me the endless supply of attention I seemed to need.

Then again, I thought, maybe it will be the same old routine. My father would never give up drinking, and as long as he didn't, life was not predictable.

I drank until I passed out.

●   ●   ●   ●   ●   ●

Despite my increasing loss of friends and health, I managed to keep passing my classes at Catholic and even got a job. Denny had left O'Rourke's to take a managerial job at the Bethesda Cinema 'n Drafthouse. The Drafthouse had been one of the grandest movie theaters in the Washington area when it opened in 1933, with a balcony and alabaster pillars running down either side. When business went south in the 1970s, it was bought by a businessman who had a remarkable idea: He would convert it into a place that showed movies and served beer. He removed the seats, leveled the floor, and put in cushioned chairs and Formica tables. In the back of the theater, behind a noise-reducing closure of glass, he built a full bar with three taps. There was also a kitchen that served pizza and sandwiches.

The idea was a huge success. Part of it was location. In the eighties, Bethesda went from being a small town that abutted Washington to a metropolitan area in its own right, with luxury hotels and one of the largest concentrations of restaurants in the area.

Denny jumped at the opportunity to work at the Drafthouse. He was tired of pulling beers—especially for guys like me who just sponged off him and gave lousy tips.

While I was happy for Denny, his new job was a potential disaster for me. I was spending what little money I had on food, and without the free drinks, I would not be able to both get drunk and eat.

In a move that was based more on friendship than wisdom, Denny's first decision as manager was to give me a job. For an alcoholic, the job was heaven. I would usually go to O'Rourke's in the afternoon and drink until five, then get on a bus to Bethesda to be at work by six. All I had to do was make sure that the kegs got changed when they blew and that the customers had their pitchers before the movie started. Then I could just pour myself a beer (which I hid in a corner of the kitchen because we weren't supposed to drink on the job), kick back, flirt with waitresses, and enjoy the movie.

I wasn't the only Prep graduate who had benefited from Denny's largess. One night when I got to work, Denny nodded toward the kitchen. "Want a shock?" he said. "Check out who the new cook is."

I went into the kitchen. Standing with his back to me, slicing tomatoes, was a guy with a military buzz cut, a leather jacket, and fatigue pants.

It was Corey Joyce, the leader of the Inquisitors and Prep's bad apple. He looked completely different. At Prep he had been a skinny kid with stringy black hair who looked like he could barely lift a kitten. Now, muscles stretched his white T-shirt, and his green eyes gleamed with intensity. He had spiked his hair and dyed it blonde.

When he saw me, he smiled and offered his hand. "Mr. Judge," he said. "What's happenin'?"

"Damn, son, where'd you get the muscles, in the army?"

"Hell no," he sneered. "I wouldn't fight for this fascist country."

"So what are you doing here?"

"Well, I was working for a socialist group, but I got fired for punching a cop."

"You *punched* a cop?"

"It was kind of an accident. We were in front of the White House protesting Reagan's policies in Central America, and this cop came at me when I wasn't expecting it. I didn't even think. I just saw this blur out of the corner of my eye and wheeled around and slugged him. There were enough witnesses who said it was an accident that I got a hundred hours of community service rather than jail time, but they canned me at the job anyway, said it would look bad. Fuckin' lightweight socialists. Nothing worse."

I smiled. "Oh, so you're a socialist now? That's not your typical career choice for a Prep graduate."

"That's 'cause Prep is full of a bunch of racist Nazis who don't give two shits about anything other than getting drunk and playing football. Most of 'em can't think and breathe at the same time." He reached under a shelf, pulled out a bottle of beer, and took a huge swig.

"Oh, I don't know if we were that stupid," I said. "We managed to roll a few houses as the Inquisitors, which takes a certain amount of tactical skill."

He belched, then laughed and shook his head. "God, the Inquisitors. I had almost forgotten about that. It fucking cost me graduation."

"Me too."

"God, what a bunch of assholes we were," he said. He slipped his beer back and grabbed a backpack off a shelf. He pulled some tapes out and began to sort through them.

"You like the Replacements?"

"The who?"

"The Replacements—the best band in America. Don't you like punk?"

I shrugged. "I never really thought about it."

He handed me a fistful of tapes. "Listen to these."

I looked at them. *Never Mind the Bollocks, Here's the Sex Pistols; The Replacements Stink; Frankenchrist.*

"I should go back to Prep and play these for Father Carmen," I said.

He waved a hand in the air. "Fuck that. They still call me asking for money. They want to build a new library and name it after Carmen. He can take every brick and shove it up his ass."

"I think he's already got a few freshmen up there," I said.

"Man, what a fascist. He should be shot." He glared at me. "You don't mean to tell me you still buy all that shit? All that Prep shit? All that Catholic religious bilge?"

I shrugged. "I don't know if I buy the religious stuff. I guess I haven't thought about it in a long time."

"That's right. None of us ever think about it. We just do it."

"Not everyone. I haven't been to church in years—since they forced us to at Prep."

"You know what Anton LaVey said about Christ?"

"Who?"

"Anton LaVey. He's a Satanist. He said, 'Christ is incompetence swinging from a tree.'"

"God, that is vile," I said.

"You ever read any Mencken?" he asked.

"Who?"

"H. L. Mencken. He was one of the most famous journalists of the twentieth century. Lived in Baltimore and wrote from the twenties to the fifties. Here," he said. He reached into his backpack and pulled out a book.

The book, *A Mencken Chrestomathy,* was a collection of favorite writings by the late journalist. Mencken was known as "the Great Debunker" and "the Sage of Baltimore." Patriotism, socialism, politicians, and religion were all topics that came under his scalpel. Later, when I got home, I began to read Corey's copy of *A Mencken Chrestomathy.* It was like stepping under a cold shower: "The argument [for creationism], once the bulwark of Christian apologetics, has been shot so full of holes that it is no wonder it has had to be abandoned," Mencken wrote. "The more, indeed, the theologian seeks to prove the wisdom and omnipotence of God by his works, the more he is dashed by the evidence of divine incompetence and stupidity that the advance of science is constantly turning up."

Mencken defined theology as "an effort to explain the unknowable by putting it into terms of the not worth knowing," called a clergyman "a ticket spectator outside the gates of hell," and referred to an Archbishop as "a Christian ecclesiastic of a rank superior to that attained by Christ."

Reading Mencken's prose, I was electrified—not only by his flippant blasphemy, but also by the power and economy of his prose. The more I read, the more my apathy about religion slowly began to turn into hostility. My father had raised me to be an intellectual, and intellectually, Mencken's arguments made sense. All religion, including my own, was just a way for humans to deal with their irrational fears, making them feel secure with childish theology. Worse, it was responsible for a lot of the violence and misery throughout history and around the world. The Inquisition. The Middle-East. Northern Ireland.

I had barely finished reading Mencken when Corey introduced me to another journalist: Hunter S. Thompson. Thompson had attained fame in the 1960s as the father of the "gonzo" school of journalism. The rules of gonzo journalism were that there were no rules; the author of an article could inject his personal life and opinions into the text, as long as he did it in a stylish, antiauthoritarian way. Thompson's style was breezy, conversational, and radical; while he blasted many targets, his main enemies were conservatives, particularly President Nixon. When Thompson heard, in 1973, that Washington Redskins coach George Allen had prayed before the superbowl and Nixon was rooting for the team, he bet against them. "I knew that any team that had both God and Richard Nixon on its side was fucked," he wrote.

Thompson was also heavily into drugs, including alcohol. His stories were chock-full of scenes of dissipation and drug intake; his masterpiece *Fear and Loathing in Las Vegas* opens with the author hallucinating while driving to Las Vegas.

Even more than Mencken, Thompson was a revelation to me. His was a journalism of a far different tack than the dry, responsible kind my father practiced. As long as it was done with some style, a journalist could be as arrogant, sarcastic, and outright partisan as he wanted, even recounting the sleazy and wild details of his own life.

This was a new kind of reporting for me, and, coupled with Mencken's blistering sarcasm, it inspired my writing more than any teacher I had ever had at Fatima or Prep. I began to submit articles to the *Tower,* Catholic's newspaper, that were written in an ersatz Thompson style. To my amazement, they ran them. The style worked particularly well when I was taking on the Catholic establishment, particularly during the Father Curran controversy.

Father Charles Curran was a priest at Catholic who had dissented from certain Vatican teachings. He supported abortion rights and sex education and, as a result, was in danger of being reprimanded by the authorities in Rome. The case became a scandal at Catholic, and when Father Curran held a press conference, I was one of the journalists from the *Tower* who attended. The conference, however, was also attended by several right-wing protesters who wanted Curran's head on a platter. A group had come from the Schiller Institute, an organization founded by the wife of the extremely conservative presidential candidate Lyndon LaRouche, and after the conference, one of their members asked me to use the paper to help bring down the apostate priest. When I turned in my piece on the conference, it was pure ersatz gonzo:

> "When bishops begin launching thunderbolts
> against heretics, the towns do not tremble;
> they laugh."
> —H. L. Mencken

I knew I was in for a good show when a seedy looking guy handed me a flyer entitled WHY IMF [Ignorant Mother Fucker] GENOCIDALISTS LOVE CURRAN'S FREE SEX, from the Schiller Institute, Inc., a knee-jerk group founded on July 4 by Helga Zepe-LaRouche, whose husband Lyndon ran for president in 1984 and accused Walter Mondale of being a KGB agent and called Henry Kissinger a Communist.

The flyer characterized CU students as "shining infants who don't like to have their freedom to masturbate challenged," and Father Curran as a defender of "the spread of infidelity, AIDS, and warts." Well, I don't have AIDS, am not married, and have never had a wart—unlike the representative who gave me the ditto, who had warts growing all over his brain. But I wasn't vexed. The fact that they were there would make Father Curran's press conference all the more enjoyable.

Curran spent the whole press conference defending his views, as was to be expected. He reinforced his support for academic freedom and the validity of dissenting from noninfallible teachings on abortion and contraception. He quoted Thomas Aquinas, "the greatest theologian in the history of the Church," on when life begins, and even accepted a challenge to debate from a member of the Schiller Institute. The whole thing was predictable, and drifted along with minimal interruption.

There was, however, a reoccurring annoyance from the second row. When Curran began to speak, a noise which sounded like a bullfrog sounding off came from somewhere near the podium. I curiously looked over, but apparently there were no amphibians in the auditorium.

Five minutes later the sound recurred; still no sign of the origin. I kept my eyes peeled in anticipation of the noise, and luckily I had my attention on a middle-aged woman in the second row as she wound up for number three: she was belching at Curran in protest.

Fine, I thought. Get the barroom bathos rolling. Fill the place with hot air. That, after all, is what the whole thing boiled down to: a bunch of blimps colliding in a stadium. . . .

After the conference I called Nicholas Benton, spokesman for the Schiller Institute, which was responsible for the flyers denouncing Curran. He had the guts to try to coax me into using the *Tower* as a tool to bring Curran to his knees by demanding a debate. "Maybe your paper can play a part in getting the debate underway," he said, "'cause we're stuck unless your paper demands that Curran makes good on his promises." I almost hung up before he finished: "Then again, students have a tendency to sit back and laugh at a controversy."

Well, I'm laughing—that's for sure. But I can see where the joke begins and ends. Anyone with a sense of the absurd can find humor in a grown woman belching in dissent or the sophomoric rhetoric of the Schiller Institute, but at the same time balk at their potential danger. People said the Nazis were a joke, and the next thing they knew their doors were being kicked in at four in the morning. Similar intolerance and military posturing surrounding the Curran controversy appropriately smacks of the hypocritical in an age when hateful men tote crosses and buckets of blood are spilt in the name of Holy jihads.

The article was genuine *faux* Thompson, from the casual, hip tone to the evocation of Nazi Germany. However, it didn't get the response I expected. A few radicals I had become friends with congratulated me on the piece, but it seemed that no one else had read it.

"Nobody gives a shit about Curran," Corey told me that night as we got drunk at O'Rourke's. "All people at Catholic care about is getting laid and Bruce fucking Springsteen."

He was right. Everyone at Catholic was too busy partying to pay attention to what was in the *Tower,* and a majority of the student body, for reasons that never became clear to me, was from

New Jersey. It was the mid-1980s and rock star Bruce Springsteen was huge everywhere, especially in the halls of Catholic. Corey hated him, preferring the punk and new wave bands whose records he bought by the armload.

When I listened to the tapes Corey kept giving me, I couldn't help but feel the same way. The bands were indeed remarkable, performing passionate, inspiring, even breathtaking music while Springsteen clunked along with his cheesy working-class anthems. Unfortunately, none of Corey's bands ever got on the radio. It was the late 1980s before the grunge explosion brought alternative American rock into the mainstream, and there was still a sense of being part of something underground and special. The Dead Kennedys, X, the Smiths, Husker Du, R.E.M., the dB's, the Church and, of course, the Replacements were only a few of the groups that didn't sell many albums but who played the music that spoke to us. The fact that such great groups were virtually unknown in the outside world was a double-edged sword. On the one hand, it let us feel smug and superior to the masses who listened to the Top 40 dreck. On the other, it drove us crazy because we thought our music was so phenomenal it should not be denied a larger audience.

Sometimes after our shift at the Drafthouse, Corey and I would go up on the roof. The Drafthouse looked over downtown Bethesda, and we would sit in a couple of lawn chairs getting drunk, talking about politics, sex, and religion, and listening to music on Corey's box. Denny had given us a key to lock up, and as long as we didn't make too much noise—it was illegal to be there drinking after two o'clock—everything was cool.

It was in these sessions that my worldview completely changed. Corey was no longer the weird loser from Prep that I had been too uptight to appreciate; he was a visionary that I was only now wise enough to appreciate. I became a radical, or as much of a radical as a well-off Catholic kid from Potomac could be. I came to believe most problems were not caused by eternal human vices like greed, envy, sloth, and decadence, but by free-market capitalism, religion, and patriotism. These were the things that kept people trapped in ignorance and fear and hindered human progress, and if we could just abolish them, we could erad-icate greed and want and usher in a golden era of intellectual achievement. These ideas, of course, were nothing new, but I was proud of the fact that my ideology was right out of the 1960s—or even the 1920s. I wanted to be the torch bearer for a new genera-tion of anarchists.

Much of this radicalism was fueled by alcohol. Had I never touched a drop of booze I very well could have been entranced by left-wing dogma, but it would not have expressed itself the same way. I probably would have spent more time trying to gather information to defend my arguments and less time making

speeches, which I was getting very good at. I also wouldn't
have been so hysterical, which was happening more and more
frequently when I drank. After a few hours on the roof or at
O'Rourke's, Corey and I could clear a room in five minutes.

One night we were up on the roof of the Drafthouse watching the stars when Corey ignited what would become the biggest
scandal of my life.

"You know," he said, "I just remembered, that fucker Bruce
Springsteen is putting out a live, five-album collection next week."

"Just in time for Thanksgiving," I said.

Corey shook his head. "All the fans are going to be lining
up like drones to get copies, and they'll probably sell ten million
of 'em. It's going to be a hideous spectacle."

"Jesus," I muttered. "What a crime against humanity."

"*That's* what you ought to write about," he said. "Rip
Springsteen a new asshole. That should get some attention."

I laughed. "I should say he's more popular than Jesus. It'll be
like the Beatles."

"You should do *something*," Corey said, tossing a bottle cap
off the roof. "Bruce Springsteen is a menace to music, and he
should be stopped."

The next week, Springsteen released his live set. As Corey
predicted, people started lining up to get the set the day before it
was out, and the event garnered blanket coverage by the media,

from the Washington *Post* to the fluffy Hollywood industry show *Entertainment Tonight*. The coverage was slavish, depicting Springsteen as not only a rock and roll icon but, with his songs of lost jobs and hard times, a hero to the average working American. He was even praised by conservative columnist George F. Will.

However, there was one editorial dissent—in the pages of the *Tower*.

> What a scene. Last Tuesday, throngs of rock 'n' roll animals lined up for miles at Tower Records, drooling like a pack of brats waiting to be breastfed. Their booty, however, was—to them—more precious than mother's milk, more valuable than Mastercard, more desirable than owning a BMW. Some hungry Georgetown students were there early to get in line, and to do so they had actually skipped class.
>
> They all, of course, were there to get a piece of the Boss, Bruce Springsteen. His new five-LP, live collection hit the racks on Tuesday, and Washingtonians descended on the record stores as if Jesus had come back and was behind the counter selling pardons.
>
> I couldn't believe my eyes when I saw them lining up on TV. What in the world? Bruce Springsteen? A live album? Five LPs? Jesus, no! Not so soon! They hadn't

even stopped playing "Born to be Overplayed" yet. I rubbed my eyes and looked again. There was no doubt about it. It was real. One guy looked just like George F. Will; then I remembered it might have *been* George F. Will. After heaping all that ignorant uninformed praise on "the Boss" in his column, maybe George was starting to dabble in rock 'n' roll, getting with it . . .

And why not? Bruce Springsteen is an all-out, teeny-bopper, pseudo-hip, bona-fide bubble-gum phenomenon now. He's thought of as a paragon of what rock 'n' roll means—a groovy spokesman for the unemployed working class. Sure, get crazy—jump in the Mercedes, pop him in the deck.

All this while the great bands are ignored. People don't like to have their illusions shattered, their tiny little worlds invaded by forces too big and ugly for their minds to handle. Springsteen has become the very rich man's rock star, shooting like a BMW through Georgetown on a Saturday night while the bus riders look on, listening to the Dead Kennedys, the Rainmakers, and of course the best band in the country—the Replacements, who make the Boss look like he should be tap dancing for a buck on the corner of Wisconsin and M.

So I guess I'll have to evade the radio for the next couple thousand years—the inane swill they pipe through it is bad enough already—until the wave, if ever, recedes. And keep reminding myself that rock isn't about *Entertainment Tonight,* it's about throwing up. And that while Bruce dances in the dark, bands like the Replacements live there.

I know, I know. No one's forcing me to listen. But no one's forcing you, either.

And I think that says it all.

The response to my article was fierce and immediate. Letters began pouring into the offices of the *Tower* calling for my head. For the only time in my college career, the letters page the following week was devoted entirely to one topic—Springsteen. "Mark Judge," one irate letter read, "how excited would you be and how long would you stand in line for a five-album set, three hours and twenty minutes, of the Replacements? Someday, your turn to stand in line will come. When it does, I hope you have a good time with it. In the meantime, please keep your seemingly limited intelligence and one-sided view to yourself. As Bruce Springsteen himself says, 'I'm only here for the fun, so what's the big deal?'" Another reader accused me of "polluting" the pages of the *Tower,* and yet another accused me of thinking I was James Dean.

It seemed as though everyone had something to say about the article, even my own family and friends. My brother Mike, the actor, had been a fervent Springsteen fan for years. He wrote to the *Tower* claiming he was "moved to dismay" by my piece. "Judge seems to think that fame negates past accomplishment, that popularity designates banality and that selling a large number of albums implies some sort of betrayal on Springsteen's part," he wrote. "Well, Cole Porter sold more songs than even the Boss has, and that enormous popularity insured that Porter's work . . . I find it hard to believe that songs like 'The River' and 'My Hometown' strike Mr. Judge as 'inane swill,' but if that's his opinion, so be it. In attacking a performer as sincere and committed as Springsteen, Judge insults only himself."

I wasn't surprised. Although only four years older, my brother had completely missed the punk, new wave, and American underground music movements of the late 1970s and 1980s, and I had expected him to defend Springsteen.

However, I didn't fully appreciate what I had done until around Christmas, when Shane and the other Catholic kids all came home for vacation.

We all met at O'Rourke's, and by ten o'clock the place was filled with familiar faces: Shane and Becky—who had stopped dating a few times since high school but always seemed to wind up together—Denny and other guys from Prep, as well as girls who had graduated from St. Catherine's, Holy Child, Visitation, and other Catholic schools.

When he saw me, Shane smiled and shook his head.

"Hey listen," he said. "I've got two things to ask you. The first is, I've got some extra tickets to see Springsteen. You interested?"

Everyone started laughing. They had heard about or read the infamous piece, even the ones who were in school on the West Coast.

"Hey man," Corey said. "Springsteen is evil. He should be deported."

"Oh, come off it," Shane said. "You guys just can't stand anyone who's popular."

What was so irritating about Shane's comment was that it was partially true. The biggest problem in the underground music scene was that people often measured authenticity by sales—if you didn't sell, you were authentic. This was a ridiculous creed that left punks open to charges that they were hypocrites, bemoaning the obscurity of their favorite bands yet turning on them as soon as they sold a few records. This led to the perception that alternative music fans would hate anything popular, no matter how good it was.

Corey and I tended to reject bands like R.E.M. that were making it big, even while we griped about them not being on the radio. Yet we honestly did hate Springsteen's music, which is why we found the adoration the Boss elicited from the masses so dispiriting.

"You know something, Shane?" Corey said, his eyes flashing with anger. "What you know about music could fit into your jock strap. You're just another one of these right-wing dumb-ass jocks who doesn't care about anything other than where his next beer is coming from. I really wish you'd just fuck off and not try to talk about things you know nothing about."

The room got quiet. Shane took a step closer to Corey, and they were face to face.

"Oh, so *I'm* the loser?" Shane barked. "Well, I've heard about you, man. You walk around in a leather jacket with that ridiculous crew cut, talkin' about a revolution. You grew up in Chevy Chase, you fucking loser, so don't try to pull that rebel-without-a-cause routine."

I was standing right next to Corey, but I just froze, not knowing what to do. I hated violence and fighting, and never knew what to do in a situation like that. It was too reminiscent of my father's unpredictable, explosive anger.

Before anyone else could step in, Corey had Shane by the throat, and they both tumbled to the floor. Corey was on top and started throwing punches, but Shane held his hand up to protect himself. Becky screamed, and Denny rushed in to pull Corey off.

"What's wrong with you?" Denny yelled at Corey, lifting him off by the collar.

Corey tried to pull loose and spat at Shane, whose lip had been split open. By now the bartender was in the middle. He took them both by the back of the neck and pushed them toward the door.

I followed them out. Becky came out behind me. She was crying. "Why didn't you stop it?" she said to me. "You were standing right there."

I just stood there in a trance.

"You're fired, Joyce." Denny said. "I never want to see you near the Drafthouse again."

"Fuck you," Corey said. He start to go after Shane again, but this time I stepped in front of him. "Come on," I said. "Get your ass into a cab." I hailed a cab and put him inside.

"Cripes, Judgie, why do you hang out with that loser?" Shane said. "He's headed nowhere fast."

"You should have never mentioned Springsteen," Becky said.

"That's right," I said. "It's all Springsteen's fault. Everything is Springsteen's fault."

Shane lifted his hand to hail a cab. "You know how I said I had two things to ask you?" he said. "Well, the Springsteen tickets were a joke. The second thing is that we're getting married in two weeks, and I want you to be in the wedding."

"Jesus, two weeks?"

"We don't want to screw around with a big noisy wedding. It's going to be a small group. It's at Blessed Sacrament, and the rehearsal dinner is at the Dubliner down on Capitol Hill."

Before I could say anything else, they were gone. I watched the cab disappear into the traffic on M street. I went back inside O'Rourke's and ordered a beer.

It wasn't until after last call, when everyone was stumbling home, that it hit me: Corey had a key to the Drafthouse. It was just like him to return there after hours for a final nightcap. And in the state he was in—drunk and angry at Denny—he would probably do something stupid.

I hailed a cab into Bethesda. I had barely stepped out the door when a plastic cup exploded at my feet, spraying beer against my legs. I jumped out of the way and looked up to the roof.

"I just sunk your battleship, asshole!" Corey hollered, shaking his fist.

"Hey, knock it off! It's me!" I called back.

He hesitated, peering closer.

"You're not Denny," he said.

"Is that who you're expecting?"

"I'm ready for him. I've got about twenty cups filled with beer for when he shows up."

*

"You're going to get arrested."

"Bring 'em on."

Another beer missile crashed at my feet. "Hey, butthead!" I yelled, "knock it off!"

Now he was laughing. He lobbed another beer at me, but I was already to the sidewalk. I came through the front door—he had left it unlocked. I locked it behind me and rushed upstairs.

By the time I reached him, we had more company. Denny had also just realized that Corey had a key and might use it, and by the time I got to the roof, he had pulled up to the front of the building and was standing on the sidewalk.

"You better give me that key and get your ass out of there *pronto.* I've already called the cops."

"Fuck you, Catholic boy," Corey sneered. Like a machine gun, he launched four cups of beer in succession. Denny dodged the first one, but the others landed on his head and chest.

"God*dammit,*" he barked, examining himself. "You are a dead man."

"Take it easy, Den," I said. "I'm trying to get him out of here."

"Who's that? Judge? I should have known you were part of this."

"I just got here," I said.

He wasn't listening. He was at the front door fumbling with his keys.

Just then, the cops arrived, pulling in behind Denny's car.

"Shit, we have to cruise," I said, tugging Corey's arm. "We're gonna get busted."

"You know, chicks love it when you get busted."

I pulled him away from the edge of the roof. Now the problem was getting to the ground. If we passed through the Drafthouse, we would run into Denny and the cops.

We rushed around the edge of the building, hunting for a way down. In the back of the building there was a dumpster. It was closed, which made the jump about twenty feet.

"We have to try it," I said. "It's our only chance."

"I'm too fucked up," Corey said.

"Bullshit."

The door to the roof crashed open.

"It's the cops," I said. "It's now or never."

"You first."

I let myself slide off the roof. I crashed onto the dumpster. My ankles rang with pain, but I hadn't broken anything. I slid to the ground.

"Come on," I called up. "You can do it."

Corey let himself go and landed with a dull clang.

"Oh fuck," he moaned.

I reached up to him. "Are you all right?"

"Yeah. But now I'm sober."

"Halt!" came a voice from the roof. "Stay right there!"

I pulled Corey off the dumpster. We fled down a street in the residential neighborhood behind the Drafthouse, then ducked behind a house.

"Jesus, it's like fleeing the SS," Corey said.

"Stupid Springsteen," I muttered. "He's the root of all evil."

We waited about a half hour, then hailed a cab and headed back to O'Rourke's. All the bartenders knew us, and whoever was working would let us in. It was going to be another all-nighter.

chapter

"I Just Want to Feel Better"

A COUPLE OF WEEKS AFTER THE NEAR ESCAPE FROM DENNY AND THE cops, I quit my job at the Drafthouse and moved into a townhouse with Corey. After six long years, I would graduate from Catholic that spring. My parents would continue to pay my rent for a few months, but they wanted me to get a decent job and pay my own way. I knew that it was probably the last time in my life that I could simply take time off and write, so I quit my job and put all my energy into writing.

Our place was in Glover Park, a neighborhood on a hill just above Georgetown. It was a longer walk to O'Rourke's than when I had lived with Denny, but only by about fifteen minutes. It was also much nicer than the old apartment. Unlike most anarchists, Corey had parents who, like mine, were paying for room and board while we were in school.

Living with Corey, it became a lot easier to express my radicalism and apostasy, which was fueled, if not entirely created, by my alcoholism. While Denny and Shane always laughed at my confrontational socialism—to them I would always be Judgie from Prep, even if I succeeded Fidel Castro—Corey fancied himself as being on the vanguard of the revolution. Unfortunately, our timing was bad. The sixties were over. It seemed that just when we were getting started, Communism was crumbling. The Berlin Wall had come down, and the Soviet Union was dissolving.

The dismantling of Communism didn't stop us, however.

Ours was a post-1960s kind of radicalism that had more to do with our own narcissism and my alcoholism than any great over-arching political philosophy or desire to help others. We rebelled primarily because of our drinking. We held ourselves apart from society, maintaining that all of our problems stemmed from a right-wing ethos of American culture. We believed that capitalism was a poison that could be redeemed with punk rock.

After moving in with Corey, I submitted articles and short stories to the *New Yorker, Esquire, GQ* and other high-paying glossies, as well as to the *Nation,* the *Progressive,* and other radical publications. Nothing sold; however, I managed to get my name in print by writing letters to the editor. I wrote to the leftist *Nation* in response to an article about Generation-X radicals and sent missives to the *City Paper,* a free weekly in Washington, bemoaning the fact that the Replacements and other great bands were never played on the radio.

After getting a few letters published, I lowered my sights on a bigger target: the Washington *Post.* During the first summer after I had graduated from Catholic, a piece appeared in the *Post's* Outlook section, which was dedicated to pundits, politicians, and cultural essays. The piece, "25 and Pending," attempted to read the zeitgeist of the "twentysomething" generation—those of us who were born after the JFK assassination and grew up "in the shadow of the baby boom." It concluded that my generation was selfish, apathetic, sarcastic, obsessed with clothes and money, and that none of this was a bad thing. As far as intellect and activism went, we simply couldn't measure up to our baby-boomer parents and siblings.

I thought the piece was outrageous. I got drunk and stayed up all night writing a five-page, single-spaced rant to the *Post,* blasting them for running such weak and superficial tripe. I argued that there were pockets of Gen-Xers who didn't care about money and who didn't listen to bad Top 40 music, and that it was people like the author who perpetuated dumb clichés about us. The next day I mailed the letter, then forgot about it.

After a few months of scraping by, I finally got a break. I was hired for forty dollars a week as an intern at the *City Paper.* The *City Paper* was Washington's answer to the *Village Voice;* it specialized in the self-consciously cool, smug, irony-drenched style of the new breed of "alternative" papers which had proliferated in the 1980s. *City Paper* was pro-choice, pro-gay rights, and heavily influenced by the punk and new wave musical movements of the late 1970s and early 1980s. The best-known writer on the paper was a rock critic who, like most rock critics, didn't know how to dance. In short, it was perfect for me.

My job was to compile calendar listings: basically, what bands were playing where. Even while I was doing this, however, I kept my eyes on bigger game. Along with the arts coverage, the

City Paper ran political stories and profiles of interesting charac-ters. Although free, it was read all over Washington, and I knew that if I could sell them a story, it could help launch a career and maybe even land me a job. Indeed, several former staffers at the paper wound up at the Washington *Post*.

Eventually, I sold the editors on an idea. It came to me when I was home having Thanksgiving dinner with my family. The table conversation, which was always loud and lively and touched on everything from the Middle East to the mythology of *Star Trek,* circled around to J. D. Salinger.

"It's amazing," my father said. "The man hasn't published anything for twenty years."

"He's also not been seen," my brother Mike added. "He keeps the press and public away like they're the plague."

"You know, that would be a great story," my mother said. "If someone could get him to talk."

It was perfect. Although there was no way I could ever hunt down Salinger, who lived in seclusion in New Hampshire, there was someone else who would make a great profile—Julian Mazor. Mazor was the author of *Washington and Baltimore* and "The Boy Who Used Foul Language," the story about the juvenile delin-quent that my father had asked me to read years before, the night he had thrown the drink in my face. Mazor was something of a folk hero in our house—a gifted writer who set his stories in

Washington, a place often overlooked by the literary world in deference to New York. Like Salinger, he had written for the *New Yorker*, then vanished. If I could find him and score an interview, it would make a wonderful story.

As it turned out, finding Mazor was easy. I simply looked in the phone book, and the first Mazor I reached was his mother. I explained that I was from the *City Paper* and wanted to interview her son.

"Gee, I don't know about that," she said. "He's a very private person. His phone number is not listed, and I'd have to call him for you."

An hour later, the response came back: he wasn't interested.

"If I could just talk to him," I pleaded with his mother. "I'm sure I could convince him to see me."

She promised to talk to him again. About an hour later, my phone rang.

"Hello, Mark Judge?" a man's voice said.

"Yes."

"This is Julian Mazor."

"Hi," I said, sitting up. "Thanks for calling me back. I guess you spoke to your mother."

"Yes, I did. Uh, I don't want to be rude, because I appreciate your interest, but I don't really do interviews."

"But I've read your book," I said. "One of my favorite

stories is 'The Boy Who Used Foul Language.' I was a lot like John, the main character, when I was growing up, and it meant a lot to me."

"Well, thank you. I appreciate that. The thing is, I'm just not a very public person."

"Well, I appreciate that. But could I just send you a copy of the paper, and you can decide after reading it? All I want you to do is think about it."

There was a long silence. "Oh, okay," he finally said. "Send me the paper and I'll think about it."

I sent him the latest issue and kept my fingers crossed. The *City Paper* boasted some very fine writers, but it also had something of a racy urban personality. While the front of the paper was politics, features, and reviews, the back was all ads for seedy rock clubs and 900 sex numbers. I enclosed a letter, detailing again how much I loved *Washington and Baltimore,* and sent it off.

In about a week, Mazor called.

"It's a very interesting paper," he said.

"Is that good or bad?"

"Oh, it's good. It's got some good writing in it."

"Does that mean you'll talk to me?"

Silence.

"I mean, we don't have to do anything you don't want. Anything you want off the record is off the record."

"Well, I'm a little nervous about getting my picture taken."

"I won't bring a photographer."

"Well . . . okay. I guess it won't hurt just to talk."

I jumped out of my chair. "Oh God, thank you, thank you. You won't regret this."

He laughed. "It's okay. But I have to warn you—I don't think I'm all that exciting."

"That doesn't matter. Can you meet me tonight?"

"Uh, tonight? Yeah, sure."

We arranged to meet at Cafe Italiano, a small restaurant in Cleveland Park, an old Washington neighborhood that surrounded Connecticut Avenue.

I got to the restaurant right on time. It was a small, homey place, with a very low ceiling and tables so close together you could whisper to the people next to you.

When I first saw Mazor, he was sitting alone at a table by the window, wearing a wool blazer and a turtleneck. He was about my dad's age and handsome, with short hair and a long, full face.

"Mr. Mazor?"

He looked up and smiled. We shook hands, and I sat down and ordered a beer.

For the next couple of hours, we talked, ate, and drank. He described Washington in the thirties and forties when he had been growing up. He immediately recognized my grandfather's name and remembered him as the great first baseman for the Washington Senators. He recounted his writing career, which began in the Air Force and led him to the *New Yorker.* When I asked him why someone so gifted had stopped publishing, he seemed to get uncomfortable.

"Well, I got married and had a couple of kids," he said. "I had other things to do."

"Lot's of writers have kids and still write," I said.

He looked at me sharply, a fork of spaghetti frozen between his plate and mouth. Then he lowered his fork and sighed.

"The main reason I stopped writing, I suppose, is that I lost the motivation."

We finished eating, and I thanked him. I jumped into a cab to go to O'Rourke's, although I probably could have sprinted there. I had pulled it off. I had gotten the story. It would be my first big byline.

I was sitting in the back of the cab thinking about the article I would write when something strange happened. I started having shortness of breath, and my hands began to tremble. The change was so abrupt it startled me, and I held my chest and tried to calm myself down.

By the time we pulled up to the front door of the bar, I was having trouble catching my breath. I ordered a shot and a beer and drank them down quickly.

Almost instantly, the symptoms vanished. Indeed, I was soon nestled in the warm glow of alcohol and ordered another round.

"Look's like you're really thirsty," a woman sitting next to me said.

I smiled and did the shot. "I just scored the interview of a lifetime."

She smiled. "Tell me about it."

We started to talk, one of those long, rambling bar conversations that touched on everything from the best kind of wood for a bar to the meaning of the universe. We bought each other several rounds of drinks, and when I looked at the clock it was after midnight.

Then, in what seemed like an instant, it was suddenly the next morning. I never left O'Rourke's before last call, but I couldn't remember a thing after I had looked at the clock. I had blacked out.

I awoke lying on my back. I looked around quickly and determined that I was in my room; then I examined myself. I was fully clothed.

I started to panic, terrified of what I could have done during the blackout. I could have done anything and not know it—I could have murdered somebody.

I called to Corey, and he appeared in my bedroom door.

"Man," he said, waving a hand in front of his face. "It smells like a fucking distillery in here."

"Were you up when I came in?"

"Yeah. You were totally gassed, kept talking about having to call someone named Ronnie."

"Ronnie? Who's that?"

He shrugged. "Probably some girl you met."

I lowered my head back onto the pillow.

I didn't know it at the time, but I had moved into the deteriorative stage of alcoholism, when tolerance begins to break down and the body begins experiencing serious side effects from the drug. I would no longer be able to drink safely. Things were about to completely fall apart.

● ● ● ● ● ● ●

The next week, the piece on Mazor was published. I got to the office of the *City Paper* at eight o'clock—an hour I hadn't seen since Prep—to get the first copies. They gave me a three-page spread with a wonderful full-page piece of art. It depicted a writer at an unplugged typewriter with a piece of paper covering his face, perfectly summing up Mazor's aborted career. I didn't read the story, afraid that I might find some mistake or be disappointed. It was enough just to look at it.

That night, I was at home writing another angry letter to the editor when the phone rang.

"Yes, can I speak with Mark Judge?"

"This is him."

"Mark, my name is Ted Sardello. I'm an editor on the Outlook page of the Washington *Post*."

I almost stopped breathing. *He had seen the story and was going to offer me a job.*

"Listen, I was calling because we got your letter. That was quite a piece of work."

"The what?"

"The letter. You know, about how all twenty-somethings aren't apathetic and the world would be a better place if the radio only played the Replacements. You wrote it a few weeks ago. Sorry it's taken so long to get back to you."

Suddenly it came back to me. He was talking about the letter I had written over the summer in response to "25 and Pending."

"Oh God, of course," I said. "I had almost completely forgotten. I thought you were calling about the *City Paper* piece I have out today."

"Uh, no, I haven't seen that, but I'll definitely look for it. Listen, I was wondering if you could come in tomorrow for a talk. Do you have any other plans?"

"No. Not at all." I was trying to sound nonchalant, but I was standing on my toes and my palms were so sweaty I could barely hold the phone.

"Great. Come by around noon."

He hung up. It was surreal—I was being offered an invitation that journalism school graduates would strangle their grandmothers for: an editor of the *Post* was so struck by something I had written that he wanted me to come down to his office.

I arrived at the lobby of the *Post* the next day at noon sharp. The receptionist buzzed up to the Outlook section, and a few minutes later the editor I had spoken with appeared in the lobby. He was in his late forties and skinny, with frizzy gray hair.

"You hungry?" he asked, shaking my hand.

"Sure."

"How's the Madison?"

"Fine," I said. The Madison hotel, across the street from the *Post,* was one of the toniest places in the city.

We went into the hotel dining room, which was just off the lobby, and ordered drinks.

"So you liked the letter?" I said.

"Well, it showed someone who was thinking."

"So did you want me to do something else?"

He leaned forward and looked me in the eye. "Let me put it this way. I think the Outlook section is dead. I think it could use some fresh voices."

"So what kind of stuff do you want me to do?"

"Anything you want."

I sat there for a few seconds, then tried again.

"But is there anything specific you think needs to be addressed? Any topics you feel—"

"Just write about anything you want."

"But can't you tell me what you're interested in as far as—"

"Look," he said. "I'm giving you *carte blanche* because I think you have potential. I'm just opening the door. What you do from here is up to you."

I nodded. I noticed that my hand had started to tremble and took a deep swig from my beer. No little shake was going to stop me. This was it. The beginning of my career. I was going to be the next Hunter Thompson.

●　　●　　●　　●　　●　　●　　●

By the time Shane's rehearsal dinner came around on Friday, everyone knew about my coup at the *Post*. The dinner was in a private upstairs room at the Dubliner, an Irish bar on Capitol Hill. Corey hadn't been invited because of his fight with Shane, so they sat me next to Denny.

"Well, you should enjoy this one," Denny said. "You're on the way to the big time at the *Post*, my man."

"Two shots of bourbon," he said. "Virginia Gentleman, if you've got it."

The waiter came back and put the shots in front of us. Denny and I clicked our glasses and fired them back.

Denny violently shook his head.

"That calls for another," I said, and ordered two more.

We did them.

"Two more," I said.

"Whoa, easy there, killer," he said. "I want to stay conscious through the dinner."

I flagged the waiter down again.

The next morning, I woke up with Denny shaking me.

"Come on, killer," he said. "Time to get up."

I had blacked out again. I didn't remember anything after doing the shots.

"Am I dead?" I whispered.

"Almost," Denny said. He was showered and dressed for the wedding, but I was still wearing my suit from the night before. It was twisted almost completely around on my body. My head hurt so much I could hardly open my eyes.

I looked around. I was in Denny's house. His parents lived on Capitol Hill, just a few blocks from the bar.

"How did I get here?"

"You passed out, and this was the closest place," he said. Then he chuckled. "You put on quite a show. After doing all those shots, you tried to get up on the table and started taking your clothes off, but Shane and I pulled you down. You also tried to make it with one of the bridesmaids."

"Jesus," I muttered. "I tried to make out with a bridesmaid? Please tell me I didn't hurt her."

"No, in the shape you were in, I don't think you could have if you had tried, and we would have stopped you. You made a serious lunge at her, then started kissing her toes. We finally just pulled you off and out of the bar. Not before you made your phone call, though."

"Phone call?"

"Yeah. You kept saying you couldn't leave without calling some guy named Ronnie."

Suddenly, it came to me. I was trying to get in touch with Ronnie, the guy from the soup kitchen. Ronnie the alcoholic.

"You called information and got this guy's number, then talked to him for about ten minutes before we left."

I got to my feet. I reached into my pocket and found a crumpled piece of paper with a number on it. I put the number in my wallet, and then I slowly peeled off all my clothes except for my boxers.

We went downstairs, and I found a gallon of orange juice in

the refrigerator and drank half of it.

It wouldn't stay down. I lurched to the sink and vomited.

"Oh, you're in bad shape, man, " Denny said. "I'll tell everyone you're too sick to come today."

"No," I said. "I have to go. It's Shane's wedding."

I looked at my hands. They were trembling.

Denny looked at the clock. "I'm going to call a cab. You sure you can make it through the wedding?"

"I think so," I said. I got up from the table and went upstairs to shower.

When I was shaving, it hit me. I felt dizzy and could hardly breathe. My heart was pounding so hard I could feel it in my toes.

The first thing I thought was that over the last few months I had somehow acquired asthma and was having an attack. My hands shook so violently that I cut myself in several places. We had suits for the wedding—snow-white shirts and bucks, navy blue blazers, and ice-cream pink ties—and the blood from my chin seeped onto my collar.

I went downstairs. "Something's wrong with me," I gasped to Denny, clutching his arm. "I think I have food poisoning or something."

"Jesus Christ," he said, "you've got blood all over your collar." He dragged me into the kitchen and splashed my neck and collar with club soda.

"You're not going to make it," he said.

"No," I snapped. "It's Shane's wedding, I can't miss it."

Our cab arrived. I tumbled outside and into the cab. The sunlight made my eyes sting.

By the time we pulled into the church parking lot, I was in a state of sheer panic. I jumped out of the cab before it had stopped and made for the sacristy in the back of the church, where I found an altar boy.

"I think I have asthma," I blurted. It was all I could think of. "You've got to help me or I'm gonna die."

He led me down a flight of stairs to the basement, a cool, dry cement room lined with smocks and candles. He gave me a glass of water.

I started pacing the floor like a boxer. I had no idea what was going on upstairs but assumed that my friends had begun seating guests. The room began to spin, and I jammed my finger down my throat in a vain attempt to make myself sick.

Denny came down the stairs. "You've got to calm down," he said, grabbing my shoulders and pushing me into a chair. "The ceremony won't start for another fifteen minutes. Just try to relax."

But I couldn't relax. I sprang up out of the chair and climbed back up the staircase. I had to get out of there. The church was filling up; it seemed as if every Irish-Catholic family in Washington was there. I had to get to the back, where the other ushers were seating people. I strolled what seemed like miles down the red aisle, waltzing past the faces of my youth. Word had gotten out that I wasn't doing well, and several people tried to pull me toward them and ask what was going on.

"Asthma," I said, without stopping.

By the time I got outside, I was so dizzy I could hardly stand.

I hailed a cab on Connecticut Avenue. By now I could hardly breathe. Whatever was happening, it was life-threatening.

"The hospital," I gasped.

I closed my eyes, and for the first time since I left Fatima, I prayed. Not a pleading prayer for God to make the suffering stop; I was sure I was far too close to death for that. I said an Act of Contrition, asking forgiveness for all my sins so that I could still have a chance of getting into heaven. *I'm sorry for what I've put my parents through,* I prayed. *I'm sorry for the people I've mistreated, for my selfishness. I'm sorry for losing my faith. Please, God, help me. It is my final hour.*

The cab was now in Bethesda. We stopped at a light, and I noticed that we were right across the street from the rescue squad.

I threw some money at the driver and jumped out.

The world was spinning. I came through the doors and fell into the arms of a woman at the front desk.

"I'm dying."

"Just take it easy," she said, putting me into a chair. She started to take my blood pressure.

"What drugs are you on?" she asked. "That will help us treat you."

"None."

"None?"

"That's right."

"Cocaine? Speed?"

"Just booze."

She didn't look convinced. Just then two volunteers came into the office.

"This guy's in bad shape with heart palpitations," she said, tearing the blood pressure machine off my arm. "We'd better take him in."

They put me on a gurney and loaded me into the ambulance, stuffing an oxygen tube up my nose.

When we got to the emergency room, a doctor hooked me up to intravenous Valium. I felt my lungs begin to open up, and a peaceful, lovely calm came over me. I was going to live. The panic attack had gone as soon as it had come.

"So," the doctor said. "What drugs do you do?"

"Excuse me?"

"Drugs. Cocaine, heroin, PCP? What are you on?"

I looked at him. This guy couldn't be for real.

"I don't do any drugs," I said.

He grunted and scribbled something on a chart.

"Do you drink?"

"Yes, but—"

"How much do you drink?"

"Uh, I have a few beers a week, I guess."

"How many is a few?"

"Three or four," I lied.

"And how often do you drink?"

"Once or twice a week," I lied again.

He scribbled some more on the chart, then let out a sigh. "Okay, here's the deal, your condition has improved, so we're sending you home. I think you might have been in withdrawal from something. If it's alcohol, then you should stop drinking."

"Wait a minute, I—"

"Get some help," he said, and was gone.

I sat up. Everyone I knew was at the wedding, and I had no way home. I pulled out my wallet and started pouring through numbers I had stashed away—girls I had gone out with, friends from the beach, the student advisor at Prep. No one who could help me.

Then a napkin from Shane's rehearsal dinner fell out and onto my lap. It said "Ronnie," and had a number scribbled on it.

It was my only chance. I had run out of options, and money.

I got off the gurney. I could breathe freely, even if I was now somewhat groggy. I wandered into the lobby and found a phone.

"Ronnie?"

"Mark. I was hoping you'd call again."

"Uh yeah, well, the reason I'm calling is I'm in kind of a pinch and—"

"I'll be right over. Where are you?"

"I'm at Suburban Hospital in Bethesda."

He hung up.

A half hour later, he pulled up in an old station wagon. I got in. He shook my hand and turned down the stereo.

"Listen, man, I really appreciate this," I said. "All my friends are at this wedding, so I had no way of getting home."

"No problem," he said.

"So how's it going?" I said. "You look sharp."

"Things are great. I got a job working at a lab, and I've re-applied to med school."

"Boy, that's great," I said.

"Hey man, miracles happen in sobriety."

"Uh-huh," I said.

"So," he said. "Do you still want to go to an AA meeting?"

I balked. "When did I say I wanted to go to a meeting?"

"Last night when you called me. But I'm guessing that you don't remember our conversation."

"No, I don't," I said. The Valium was making me so loose, I didn't have the energy to lie.

"You called me last night and asked me to come out and talk to you. You told me you thought you were an alcoholic. You took a very important step, Mark, even if you don't remember it. You admitted that you have a problem."

I didn't say anything.

"Listen," he said. "I know you've had a rough day, but I'm on my way to a meeting now, and I'll take you along if you want to go. If not, I'll be happy just to drop you home."

"Whatever."

"Whatever what? Whatever let's go to the meeting, or whatever take me home?"

"The meeting."

I couldn't believe what I was saying. Of course, I told myself that I was only doing this out of curiosity, that there might even be a story in it. I was just doing it for the hell of it and to avoid going home and facing everyone's questions about where I had disappeared to.

The AA meeting was just around the corner, in the basement of an office building in Bethesda. The room was about half full with people of all ages, sexes, and colors. In the front of the room there was an old green sofa, and on it sat a black guy who looked like he was around forty. He wore a suit, like he had just come from work.

As we sat down, he pulled a piece of paper out of his pocket and started to read the AA Preamble.

Alcoholics Anonymous is a fellowship of men and women who share their experience, strength and hope with each other that they may solve their common problem and help others to recover from alcoholism.

The only requirement for membership is a desire to stop drinking. There are no dues or fees for A.A. membership; we are self-supporting through our own contributions. A.A. is not allied with any sect, denomination, politics, organization or institution; does not wish to engage in any controversy; neither endorses nor opposes any causes. Our primary purpose is to stay sober and help other alcoholics achieve sobriety.

He stopped reading and looked up. "Hi," he said. "My name is Craig and I'm an alcoholic."

"Hi, Craig!" everyone said in unison.

"I want to hear everyone else share, so I'll keep my story to a minimum. Besides, I think most of you have heard me lead before.

"I grew up in Brooklyn, New York, and alcohol was a part of my life right from the beginning. My parents got divorced when I was in high school, in large part because my father was an alcoholic. He was a mechanic, and my mother was a housewife. Like a lot of alcoholics, my father never missed a day of work. He also never missed a cocktail. He used to call us from the city and say he was going out for a drink after work and would be home in an hour, and we wouldn't see him until the next morning."

Heads around the room nodded. These people had done the same thing.

"It's funny, though," Craig said. "He never missed a day of work. Growing up I always thought that alcoholics were these people who lived on the street and could barely stand, much less work. I had no idea how pervasive this disease is."

"From Yale to jail," Ronnie whispered.

"Anyway, when I was thirteen I got drunk for the first time. My parents had gone to some party in Manhattan, and my best friend, Jimmy Luper, and I got into the liquor cabinet and fixed ourselves screwdrivers.

"I'll never forget that first drink. It was like somebody had flicked a switch and turned the world on. Suddenly, I didn't feel pain anymore. I remember it was a hot summer night, and Jimmy and I went out pool-hopping—you know, where you jump fences and go swimming at houses where no one's home? We had a great time, but by the time we got to the last pool I was sick. I threw up right in the deep end, then passed out. Jimmy had to call my parents to come get me.

"Despite getting sick, I didn't learn my lesson. When my parents were going through their divorce, I would just go into the city and stay with a friend, and we would buy beer illegally and get drunk. One time I passed out on the subway, when I came to I was in a really bad part of town. I was robbed and beaten, and the cops had to bring me home. My parents were so freaked out, they never even asked me what had happened. I just told them that I had been walking down the street and these guys had jumped me. I didn't mention that I had passed out.

"Through some miracle, I managed to make it through trade school and learned how to be a mechanic. It was just after getting out of school that I met the girl I would fall in love with and wind up coming down to Washington to live with.

"When I got to Washington, my alcoholism really progressed. My girlfriend and I got married, but the wedding was a disaster because I got drunk and passed out at the reception. The marriage wasn't much better. I was going to bars every night and began to black out when I drank. My wife would always find me passed out on the front stoop. I showed up for work drunk and was fired.

"After about a year of this, my wife finally decided that she had had enough. She told me either I could get some help for my drinking or she was leaving. I tried to stop on my own, but it never worked. I tried yoga and therapy and vitamins—nothing helped. I remember reading in a health magazine that someone in Sweden was claiming that carrots cured alcoholism, and I went out and bought about ten pounds of carrots. I ate carrots for two days, and by the third day I was drunk again.

"Finally, three years ago, I hit bottom. My wife left, and I got evicted from our apartment. I remember the night I got booted, I went to bar; I had about ten dollars to my name. I drank about fifty dollars' worth of booze, and when I couldn't pay I tried to run. They got me and called the cops, and when I resisted arrest I spent the night in jail.

"It was in that jail cell that I finally asked God for help. I knew that I was at the end of the line, that if I kept it up I would be dead or in prison for the rest of my life. I actually got on my knees right there in my cell—I was lucky no one else was there—and prayed to God to help me. I promised that I would do anything to stop the cycle.

"When I got out, I went to my first AA meeting. It was in a tiny room in an old building downtown, and my first thought was that all these people were losers. Still, I stayed for the meeting. And when the leader told her story, something strange happened. I began to identify with what she was saying. The leader was a white woman from the suburbs who was about twice my age, but she was talking about things I could understand. She knew about cravings and blackouts. She understood the awful despair of not being able to stop, the depression of being alone and addicted. She knew about alcoholism.

"After the meeting, I introduced myself to her and asked her if she would help me. She gave me her number and said she'd take me to any meetings I wanted, but that it was tradition to have a sponsor of the same sex. We went to meetings together for a couple weeks until I met a guy who I thought would make a good sponsor. I've been sober ever since.

"The thing that has kept me sober is the simplicity of AA. That's really the most amazing thing—it's so simple! I mean, all I have to do is not drink, go to meetings, and say my prayers, and I will earn a daily reprieve from my obsession to drink. Because in the meetings I learn tools that help me stay sober. I learn how to live one day at a time. I also learn how to let things go and admit it when I'm powerless over something. I learn that God's in charge and I'm not, and that all I have to do is turn my life and my will over to Him and I can achieve some sense of serenity."

After Craig finished telling his story, he began to randomly pick people, who would spend a few minutes talking about their own experiences.

My heart began to pound. *Whatever happens,* I thought, *don't let him pick me.*

After a few people had spoken, he pointed at me.

"Me?" I said.

He smiled and nodded.

"Uh, I don't even know if I belong here," I babbled. "I've never been to an AA meeting before."

The room erupted in applause. "Welcome," everyone called out. The guy behind me patted me on the back.

I smiled, feeling like a fool. "Thanks," I said. "But I have nothing to say."

"So what did you think?" Ronnie said as we drove home after the meeting.

"It was weird," I said. "I could really identify with everything that guy was talking about."

"So you think you're an alcoholic?"

I opened my mouth to answer, but no words came out. Instead, I started to cry.

I was an alcoholic. There was no denying it anymore.

"It's okay, man," Ronnie said, patting me gently on the back. "I understand."

"I just want to feel better," I said.

"You will," he said. "It takes time. But you've made the first move. You've surrendered."

We drove into Georgetown and pulled up to my townhouse.

"Here, take this," he said. He handed me a small, thick blue paperback. "It's the Big Book of Alcoholics Anonymous. You might want to read it."

I looked at the book, then at him. "My days of having fun are over, aren't they?"

He laughed. "I think they might just be beginning. Who knows, you might even wind up swing dancing."

I got out of the car, then turned around. "One more thing," I said. "I don't believe in God."

He laughed again. "Just keep coming to meetings," he said, and pulled away.

When I got home, there was a message on the answering machine from Denny. "Hey Judgie, what happened? You just kind of disappeared, and everyone was wondering if you were all right. Listen, I'm having a little Prep reunion next month, on the tenth. I've invited all the guys from our class, and it's going to be at O'Rourke's. It starts at eight o'clock, so be there."

chapter

Giving Up the Sauce

FOR THE NEXT COUPLE OF WEEKS, I WENT TO AA MEETINGS EVERY day. While I didn't mention the meetings to Corey and the other Prep guys, I did tell them that I was giving up the sauce for a while. They didn't even think twice about it. In the community we had been raised in, tales of people drying out for brief periods of time were common. After a particularly bad episode at a party or the beach, the offender would go underground for a few weeks then reemerge with a thirst as great as ever. It was a form of penance.

However, I realized that my case involves never coming out of retirement. The panic attack that had smitten me at the wedding had terrified me, and I knew that there was something wrong with me and that it had to do with alcohol.

Furthermore, I was actually beginning to like AA. There is a magic that occurs in the sixty minutes of an AA meeting that's hard to define. From the outside, a bunch of people sitting around talking about drinking and life and spirituality seems like slow purgatory, but whenever I went to a meeting, I inevitably felt better when I walked out. A large part of it was the humor of the other alcoholics, who, while acknowledging the tragedy of alcoholism and its pernicious effects on the soul, mind, and body, nonetheless knew that very funny things often happened to us when we were drunk. They also didn't deny the blissful, sexy, romantic feeling that alcohol gave us.

Indeed, I soon came to feel like I belonged in AA. Whether because of God, camaraderie, or what one alcoholic called the "spiritual ether" of the rooms, at these meetings I experienced the kind of belonging I had only felt during the best times with the Prep guys. It was a warm sense of being with people who knew you better than anyone else. In an odd paradox that is common among religious traditions that advise subjugating the ego to attain happiness, AA, with its emphasis on humiliation, gratitude, and working the Steps, imbued life with joy. Ultimately, it was an affirmation of life as being good and worth living.

However, despite the daily meetings, which only provided a brief respite, my health was not improving. I was getting to know other drunks, but no amount of support seemed to be able to help with a problem I had never before suffered from: depression.

It began almost as soon as I had stopped drinking. Although I was sober, I couldn't have been more miserable. I barely made it through a day without horrible headaches. I avoided Corey and the other guys, locking myself in my room and listening to music whenever people were around and telling them that I was sick. When I did try to leave the house, panic attacks would often drive me back to the shelter of my room. I did manage to get to AA meetings, but only those in Georgetown that I could walk to. I never felt comfortable more than a few blocks from my house.

I read about depression, but the descriptions—of the sluggish physical feelings, the wet blanket that seems to cover the brain and spirit, the desire to commit suicide not for any urge to die but to end the suffering—always fell short of capturing the dark recesses that I was enduring.

Things continued to get worse. There were days when I didn't even get dressed, staying in my room all day drinking sodas and watching TV. I only left my room for meetings or for food. I had read in an AA book that eating something sweet could stave off a craving, and I gorged myself on cookies and ice cream.

I kept the shades drawn because the sunlight hurt my eyes and left the TV on all the time. My only relief came when I convinced myself that if things got too bad I would check in at St. Elizabeth's, the mental hospital, and throw myself at their mercy before trying to commit suicide.

When I talked about my depression in AA meetings or to Ronnie, he told me to "keep coming back" and introduced me to other drunks who had gone through or were going through the exact same thing. They advised me to stick to the program and "work the Steps." Working the Steps, however, didn't have any effect. Even when I admitted that I was powerless over alcohol, I had headaches. When I handed the problem over to a Power greater than myself—in my case, it was the AA group because I still didn't believe in God—it did nothing to stop my despondency. I explained to Ronnie what I found baffling about my malady: that it didn't seem to be contingent upon any factors in life. I was depressed whether I was getting a rejection letter from a magazine I had submitted a story to or being told by my editor at the *Post* that he had loved my piece about Julian Mazor.

While Corey was out getting drunk, I hunkered down at home, burying myself in *Alcoholics Anonymous,* the Big Book of AA that Ronnie had given me.

First published in 1939—four years after the founding of AA—*Alcoholics Anonymous* is composed of hair-raising accounts of alcoholics who endured the misery of morning jitters, DT's, and draconian Depression-era rehabs before being saved by AA. The book recounts the story of AA co-founder Bill Wilson. Wilson went from the fast track of a New York stockbroker in the 1920s to alcoholic debauchery in the 1930s, winding up in the hospital with the diagnosis that he was "hopeless" and would probably have to be institutionalized. While in the hospital, Wilson was visited by a friend, Ebby T., who claimed to have gotten sober by having a religious conversion and handing his problem over to God. The friend left Wilson a copy of William James's *The Varieties of Religious Experience;* Wilson read the book, learning that many spiritual conversions have something in common: absolute despair and deflation of the human ego often precede them.

Still, Wilson found it hard to humble himself and slipped into a deep depression. He would later describe what happened next:

My depression deepened unbearably and finally it seemed to me as though I were at the bottom of the pit. I still gagged badly on the notion of a Power greater than myself, but finally, just for the moment, the vestige of my proud obstinacy was crushed. All at once I found myself crying out, "If there is a God, let Him show Himself! I am ready to do anything, anything!"

Suddenly the room lit up with a great white light. I was caught up into an ecstasy which there are no words to describe. It seemed to me, in the mind's eye, that I was on a mountain and that a wind not of air but spirit was blowing. And then it burst upon me that I was a free man. Slowly the ecstasy subsided. I lay on the bed, but now for a time I was in another world, a new world of consciousness. All about me and through me there was a wonderful feeling of Presence, and I thought to myself, "So this is the God of the preachers!" A great peace stole over me and I thought, "No matter how wrong things seem to be, they are right. Things are all right with God and His world."[1]

After getting out of the hospital, Wilson set off "on jet propulsion" to cure other drunks. But despite his conversion, he was still plagued by cravings. In 1935, while staying in a hotel in

Akron, Ohio, his thirst grew so powerful that he called a church and asked to be put in touch with an alcoholic—after all, if nothing else, preaching to other alcoholics had kept Wilson himself sober. Wilson was referred to Dr. Bob Smith, an alcoholic physician. The meeting, which took place on Mother's Day, 1935, convinced the two men that alcoholics who couldn't stay sober separately could do so together. AA was born.

Wilson's experiences led him to conclude that the only way to stay sober was by deflating the ego, which he believed was largely responsible for the will to drink. Borrowing from various religions, Wilson wrote the Twelve Steps of Alcoholics Anonymous, which encourage alcoholics to "turn our will and our lives over to God," make "a fearless and searching moral inventory," make amends to all the people we hurt in the past, and live a more conscientious, humble, and spiritual life dedicated to God and helping other alcoholics.

After reading the Big Book, I went on to read the other books about AA—*Not God, 'Pass It On,' Bill W., Dr. Bob and the Oldtimers.* Through this reading, I discovered that after he had gotten sober, Wilson became interested in consciousness and mystical experiences, and eventually tried LSD.

After meeting author and philosopher Aldous Huxley in 1943—Huxley would later call Wilson "the greatest social architect of the century"—Wilson was introduced to two psychiatrists,

Humphrey Osmond and Abram Hoffer, who were treating alcoholics with the experimental drug lysergic acid diethylamide—LSD. Although he initially expressed disdain for the experiments—he was against using any drugs in the treatment of alcoholics—he relented and eventually supported the experiments after learning about the results the psychiatrists were getting. "It is a generally acknowledged fact in spiritual development that ego reduction makes the influx of God's grace possible," Wilson wrote. "If, therefore, under LSD we can have a temporary reduction, so that we can better see what we are and where we are going—well, that might be of some help." [2]

Wilson jumped at the chance to try LSD. Here was a chemical that could provide the "deflation at depth" of the ego, the "hitting bottom," that Wilson believed was necessary to recover. In August 1956 Wilson dropped acid in California, under the supervision of psychiatrist Sidney Cohen. Wilson was enthusiastic about the experience; according to 'Pass It On,' he "felt [LSD] helped him eliminate many barriers erected by the self, or ego, that stand in the way of one's direct experience of the cosmos and of God." Two years later Wilson wrote down observations comparing an LSD trip to spiritual states: "[There is] the probability that prayer, fasting, meditation, despair, and other conditions that predispose one to classic mystical experiences do have their chemical components." [3]

I was intrigued by Wilson's experience with LSD. He seemed
to be saying that many states of mind were chemically based.
Because my depression had physical symptoms such as headaches
and dizziness, I thought there might be something biochemical
going on in my body, and that, as such, it was a problem that
could be relieved with medication. Maybe my alcoholism was
chemically based.

Finally, after being sober about a month, I decided to see an
addictions counselor. Her name was Dr. Ryan, and I had gotten
her name from Ronnie. Her office was on Connecticut Avenue
near Dupont Circle, an artsy and bohemian section of Washington.

Dr. Ryan was tall and skinny, with a fair complexion and
large square glasses. She exuded cool confidence, shaking my hand
when I came in to her office and smiling warmly.

"Mark? How *are* you?" she said, offering me her hand. I
stood and took it, then we both sat down.

I glanced at the clock. "I'm here because I'm depressed," I
said. I only had an hour and it was costing me a hundred bucks, so
I wanted to cut right to the chase.

She nodded sympathetically and seemed to appreciate that I
was no-nonsense. "Why don't you tell me when it started."

"Just in the last few weeks, since I stopped drinking." I told
her about the blackouts, the wedding, the panic attacks. Then I
went back to the summer I had started drinking with Seamus

and recounted how my drinking had slowly gotten out of hand.

She sat there, nodding and taking notes. I must have blabbed for about a half hour without taking a breath. I was broke, and this could be my only shot at therapy. I wanted to get my money's worth.

Finally, I stopped. She sat there for a few seconds scribbling, then put her pen down.

"Tell me," she said. "Do you think you're an alcoholic?"

I laughed. "Of course. But if being sober means being this depressed, then I'd rather be drunk."

"Well, Mark, it takes time to achieve a solid sobriety. Physically and emotionally, you're just starting to gain your sea legs."

"I just wish this had never happened. I wish I could just go back to a few years ago, when everything was great."

She looked sad. "I'm afraid that is not possible, at least on the basis of what you've told me so far. It sounds like you're an alcoholic, and alcoholics can't drink safely. It's not about willpower or character. Alcoholism is a disease. If you are an alcoholic, you're physically different from others. You react to alcohol in a different way."

"But how did I get this way?"

"The causes of alcoholism are multifaceted. We know what the symptoms are, namely, a physiological and emotional dependence on the drug, but even the NIAAA—that's the National Institute of Alcohol and Alcohol Abuse—hasn't been able to pin down a definite cause in every case. It's a complicated mix of genetics, environment, psychology, and culture. You might have been born predisposed to be an alcoholic and just needed a drink to push the button. One thing you can do is look at your family to see if there's a history of alcoholism. Why don't you tell me about your parents. Do they drink a lot?"

I looked at her sharply. The last thing I wanted to turn this into was a session of bashing my folks.

"My parents are fine," I said.

"Do they drink?"

"Yes."

"A lot?"

"My father does. Every night."

"Do you get along with him?"

"Sure," I said. "I mean, I think we're very different people and we've had run-ins over the years, but I don't think it's anything out of the ordinary. Anyway, I don't see what that has to do with—"

"Tell me about them, about your conflicts."

I began to squirm. While my relationship with my father had certainly had its ups and downs, he was not the villain in this. He was certainly not the reason I was depressed.

Reluctantly, I told her about some of the fights we've had. She nodded and wrote in her pad.

"But I wasn't depressed until I stopped drinking," I said. "I don't think it has anything to do with my father. I think it has to do with alcohol. Maybe it's even chemical."

"Are you undergoing any treatment right now? A rehab?"

"No. Just AA."

"AA is a good start. Keep going. You might also want to look into a treatment program."

I just nodded. I didn't want to tell her I couldn't afford it.

"If I can't get into treatment right away, what do I do about these damned panic attacks?" I asked. "I can barely function with them."

"Your depression as well as the panic may be related to your drinking. That needs to be evaluated as you continue to abstain from alcohol. In the meantime, I'm going to prescribe a tranquilizer for your panic. But it's a very small prescription. It's just for emergencies and to tide you over until you can get some more help."

The words weren't even out of her mouth when I felt a rush of relief, and shock. Tranquilizers. Of course. I didn't have to live in fear of leaving the house and getting a panic attack. I could carry tranqs. It was so simple.

For the next few days, I went to meetings at least once and

sometimes three times a day. I shared at every one, revealing my frustrations about not being able to impress my father, and how alcohol helped me deal—or rather not deal—with this in high school and college. I was working the Steps to stay sober, but I was anxious to get to the root of what had made me a drunk. I shamelessly dug into every relationship and conflict I had ever had. I recalled my party and how I had dumped Mary for Laura. I relived the Drafthouse days and admitted that Corey was a bad influence and most likely an alcoholic.

I read everything I could get my hands on about alcoholism, taking stacks of books on the subject home from the library. I particularly liked ones that had to do with writers. One of my favorites was Jack London's *John Barleycorn, or Alcoholic Memoirs,* which reflected my own story. London started drinking as a young sailor in San Francisco, and after several years he began to lose control. He suffered from panic attacks and suicidal depression. "The things I had fought for and burned my midnight oil for, had failed me," he wrote. "Success—I despised it. Recognition—it was dead ashes. Society, men and women above the ruck and the muck of the water-front and the forecastle—I was appalled by their unlovely mental mediocrity. Love of woman—it was like all the rest. . . . Art, culture—in the face of the iron facts of biology such things were ridiculous, the exponents of such things only the more ridiculous."

I wondered what London could have meant by "the iron facts of biology." He seemed to be saying that his depression was chemically based, and therefore aesthetics, environment, and personality could do nothing to change it.

After *John Barleycorn,* I read another book that made me question the idea that my alcoholism had an environmental or psychological basis—indeed, made me question whether any cases of alcoholism are purely psychological. It is called *The Thirsty Muse: Alcohol and the American Writer,* written by British journalist Tom Dardis. *The Thirsty Muse* dismantles the myth that America's great writers achieved that greatness in part because of their drinking. Profiling Hemingway, Faulkner, O'Neill, and Fitzgerald, Dardis argues that alcoholism actually destroyed the talent of most of these men and cut their careers short. The one who escaped, Eugene O'Neill, got sober and stayed that way for twenty years, during which time he wrote *The Iceman Cometh* and *Long Days Journey into Night,* his two finest plays.

According to Dardis, alcoholism is a purely biological disease whose onset has nothing to do with personality:

> Faulkner's principle biographer, Joseph Blotner, ascribes his subject's heavy drinking to his need for temporary oblivion from the world around him. Blotner views the prolonged binges as experiences that Faulkner chose of

his own accord, something *willed*. Yet it is clear that Faulkner did *not* will his binges—they were far too painful and damaging for that. He was always surprised to find himself back in the hospital. The bouts of drinking were, in effect, the inevitable result of a disease over which he had little or no control.[4]

"Most alcoholics do not drink because they are emotionally ill to begin with," Dardis concluded. "*They drink because they're alcoholics;* the psychological disorders follow." (Emphasis in the original.)

I would soon come to agree with Dardis, with one addendum: It is all, not most, alcoholics whose illness is triggered by biology and not psychology.

When I told Ronnie about what I had learned, he just shrugged. He thought my problem was that I didn't know how to have sober fun. He kept insisting that I go dancing with him and Ruth.

Finally, I decided to go. The place where they danced was called the Spanish Ballroom. It was part of Glen Echo, an old amusement park that stood on a hill in the woods above the Potomac River. Glen Echo had been a built in the 1930s; as a child, my father had gone there to ride the carousel. It closed in the 1960s, but the ballroom was still open. It was an airy, cavernous space, about as big as a small airplane hangar and large enough to comfortably hold 500 dancers. It had no heat or air-conditioning, but it was early May and the night was cool and cloudless.

When I walked into the ballroom, it was like stepping back in time. There was a twenty-piece big band, the Tom Cunningham Orchestra, on the stage, and they produced a sound unlike anything I had ever heard. My dad used to play big band records, but those were recordings made with primitive technology. It was quite different live. You could feel the rhythm of the drummer and the blast of the horn in your entire body, and the players were right in front of you, close enough to touch. It was a different world from the mega concerts I had grown up on, where you needed binoculars to see the band.

The smooth wooden floor was filled with couples swing dancing. They moved side to side and back together, a mirror image of each other. A man lifted his arm and the woman twirled under, then they effortlessly snapped back to their original position, always moving.

Ronnie had told me that closer to the stage was where the really great dancers performed. It was here that you saw the best moves, including serials, where the man would toss his partner over his shoulder or slide her between his legs.

Ronnie and Ruth were standing in the corner watching the dancers.

"Hey, twinkle toes," I said.

"I don't believe it," he said, taking my hand. "Lazarus has risen! I thought for sure you'd chicken out."

"Me? How could you think such a thing?"

"Because everyone your age is terrified of learning how to dance right," he said. "Everyone's too self-conscious. This requires that you *let go* a little bit. And for your generation—and especially for alcoholics—letting go it not easy."

"Hey, I have no shame," I said. "I'm willing to try something new."

He turned to Ruth. "Hey Mom, can you show Mark the basic swing step?"

Ruth got up and took my hand, leading me onto the dance floor.

"Can you count to six?" she said.

"It's been a while, but I think I can hack it," I said.

"Okay, hold me," she said.

I took her right hand in my left hand and wrapped my right hand around her back.

"Now let's try the basic step," she said. "Step left on one-two, right on three-four, then back and forward on five-six."

I lunged to my left.

"No no no," she said, pulling me back to the center. "Take small steps, like walking."

I took small steps. She held me tightly so I wouldn't lose track, and we slowly moved around the floor.

"You got it," she said.

I did. We moved together in perfect time to the band. She went under for a turn and snapped back. I was dancing. Ruth smiled at me.

"This is actually just a piece of the larger dance, the Lindy Hop," she said. "It was named after Charles Lindbergh, who hopped across the Atlantic in 1927. The Lindy Hop is eight counts and much more complicated than this. I'll show it to you when you get used to this."

I turned her under my arm again, and smiled. This was actually fun.

Then it hit me. The panic. My lungs seemed to shut down, and the room began to spin. I stopped dancing.

"You okay?" Ruth said.

"It's okay," I stammered. "I just have to take some medicine."

I reached into my pocket.

It was empty. I had left the tranquilizers back at my apartment.

I told myself not to freak out, but it was too late. I was already hyperventilating.

"I have to go," I said. "I left some medicine at my apartment, and I have to go back and get it."

"Oh, okay," Ruth said, looking a little confused. "When you get it, come on back."

I ran outside. *If I don't get a tranquilizer in the next few minutes, I'm going to die,* I thought. There was no way I could make it all the way back to Georgetown to get my pills. I had to face it. It was time to call an ambulance.

I rushed over to a convenience store located in a small shopping center across the street from Glen Echo.

"I need the phone," I said.

"Two doors down," the clerk said. "In front of the liquor store."

Liquor store. As soon as the words were out of his mouth, I knew I was about to drink again. I had no desire to get drunk, but it was the only thing that could save my life. If I could get drunk fast and pass out, it would prevent me from choking to death while I waited for an ambulance.

I marched inside the store and bought a pint of bourbon. Then I went around to the back of the building, opened it, and drank half of it down.

Relief came quickly. My toes started to tingle, then the feeling moved up through the rest of my body. My lungs loosened up. I took another couple hits off the bottle, then tossed it aside.

Suddenly, I was overcome with shame. I hadn't wanted to drink, and while I now felt at ease, I knew that if I went in and got another bottle, I would wind up in a blackout, or worse.

I realized that I needed help right away, or I wasn't going to make it. I needed to go to a rehab. I decided to go home and talk to my parents, who were paying my insurance. I needed to tell them the truth: I was an alcoholic and it was life-threatening. I needed help, starting tonight.

I picked up the bottle and finished it. Then I drove out of Washington and Potomac, with each mile my breath becoming more assured, the calmness taking over my body.

I was almost home when I noticed, on a hill above the road, a familiar sight: Our Lady of Fatima, my old grade school. For some reason, I pulled into the parking lot. I wasn't struck with any deep religious feelings; I was returning to Fatima out of sheer cowardice. I was afraid I was going to die and wanted to square myself with God if I was on my way out. When it came down to it, all my atheistic ranting was just that—empty blathering by a spoiled brat who had been given everything in life and had never known real adversity. It was easy to be an atheist during happy hour at O'Rourke's, with Corey egging me on and parents who were able to bail me out of any mess I got myself into. But now I had an affliction that money, sarcasm, and, most important, alcohol, couldn't cure. I was out of options.

Slowly, I entered the church. I hadn't been in here since I was a student at Fatima. I remembered walking down this red carpet during my first communion, waiting in the pews to make my first confession, feeling chills during the Stations of the Cross.

I was almost to the front when I saw the priest on the altar—Father Paul, the man who had been my spiritual guide at Fatima.

For a few seconds I just watched him. Then I came up to the edge of the altar.

"Excuse me, Father Paul," I said. "I was wondering if I could make a confess—"

I started sobbing. It was as if everything that had happened in the last few months hit me at once. I started to crumble and would have hit the floor had he not caught me.

"Easy there, easy," he said, helping me into a pew. He held me while I shook, the sound echoing in the empty building.

He handed me a handkerchief. "Just try to settle down," he said. "Just take it easy."

"I'm dying," I whispered.

"It's okay," he said. "I'm here, Mark."

He remembered me.

"I'm a drunk," I said. "A drunk who rejected God."

"It's all right, Mark. Just take it easy. Breathe deep."

I began to breathe deeply and slowly regained my composure.

I told him about everything that had happened, about the panic attacks, the blackouts. He listened intently, nodding at different times.

"We can get you some help," he said. "Wait here."

He left and returned a few minutes later, carrying a magazine and a small book.

"Are you in AA?" he asked.

I nodded.

"Good. Keep going, as often as possible." He handed me the book and magazine. "Read these. I used to do some alcoholism counseling, and the man who wrote this book is the most knowledgeable person working in the field today. It will give you some of the information you don't get in AA. You also need to be in treatment."

"I'm going home to talk to my parents about that right now."

"Good. Remember, you can always reach me here. Use the church as an anchor. If you want to come in and pray, at any hour, let me know and I'll open it up."

"Thank you, Father," I said. He headed out the door, pausing only long enough to bless himself with holy water.

After the door had shut behind him, I got on my knees. I closed my eyes and said a Hail Mary and an Our Father, then spoke to God. I asked Him to give me courage and strength and to forgive me my sins. While I was praying I felt a faint sense of calm, the kind of tranquillity I hadn't experienced in years—probably since before I had started to drink.

When I got home, my parents were watching television. My father was drinking out of a tumbler.

"Can you turn the TV off?" I said. "I have something to tell you."

I sat in front of them. "I'm an alcoholic," I said. "And I need some help. I need to go to a rehab."

They sat there silent for a few seconds.

"What makes you think you're an alcoholic?" my father said.

I knew I should have waited until morning. It was after five, and Dad had already had a few.

Slowly and carefully, I recounted everything that had happened in the last year. My parents listened, looking uncomfortable.

When I had finished, my father just shook his head, as if I had just blown a play during a crucial game. "Look," he said. "I'm not paying for any rehab. There was a writer at the *Geographic* who was a drunk, and we sent him to rehab. When he came back, he was drunk again before he got off the plane."

I just sat there, examining my hands. My mother said nothing.

"Do you have a girlfriend?" my father asked.

"No," I whispered.

"That's your problem. You need a girlfriend. Then you wouldn't have to go out and drink all the time. A good woman would keep you out of the bars." He got up and walked out of the room. I heard the door to his den shut behind him.

I left the room, then climbed upstairs. I wanted to go back to Georgetown but was too exhausted. I got into my old bed and started to look at the material Father Paul had given me: a magazine article called "The Alcoholism Revolution," and a book called *Under the Influence: A Guide to the Myths and Realities of Alcoholism*. Both were written by a clinical psychologist named James Milam.

My ideas about alcoholism were about to be turned upside down.

chapter

Choose Life

THE NEXT MORNING, I LEFT BEFORE MY PARENTS WERE UP. I
returned to my apartment, where I locked myself in my room,
and started to read.

According to the author of the material, Dr. James Milam,
alcoholism is caused primarily by biological factors. Milam claims
that alcoholics are born with a set of biological factors that set
them up for addiction even before they touch a drop. In alcoholics, enzymes, brain waves, genetics, prenatal influences, and
adaptations in the metabolism and central nervous system all act,
either separately or in combination, to produce a reaction to the
drug that is markedly different from that of normal drinkers.
These predrinking differences are responsible for an increase in
tolerance for the drug, which drives the alcoholic to increase
drinking; in other words, alcoholism causes heavy drinking, not
the other way around. Milam describes this in *Under the Influence.*

> Two major misconceptions about the phenomenon of
> tolerance should be straightened out. The first is the
> belief that tolerance is a learned response. Many people
> think that the more the alcoholic drinks, the more he
> learns how to compensate for the effects of drinking.
> But tolerance is not learned, nor is it subject to the
> alcoholic's conscious control or willpower. Tolerance is
> caused by physiological changes which occur primarily

in the liver and central nervous system. These changes cause alterations in the alcoholic's brain's electrical impulses, its hormone and enzyme levels, and the chemical structure of cell membranes, all of which contribute to tolerance. Learned behavior cannot possibly account for these physiological and biochemical functions.

The second and very misleading misconception is that tolerance initially develops because the person drinks too much. Many alcoholism theorists and professionals insist that psychological or emotional problems are the cause of increased drinking; as the person drinks more frequently, they conclude, he runs the risk of becoming tolerant to alcohol. Again, the implication is that alcoholics are responsible for contracting their disease—by drinking too much, they make themselves tolerant to alcohol. Yet the opposite is true. Tolerance is actually responsible for the alcoholic's continued and increasingly large intake of alcohol. In fact, an increase in the amount and frequency of drinking is the typical symptom of a developing tolerance to alcohol and one of the first warning signs of alcoholism.[1]

When I read those words, it was like watching the earth go from flat to round. Milam was saying that popular perceptions about alcoholism were not slightly off or somewhat misguided, but wrong. And his argument made sense. I hadn't become an alcoholic when I went to Catholic or got a job at the Drafthouse or had my interview at the *Post*. Alcoholism had been working in me since the night on that beach years ago when I got drunk with Seamus. My skyrocketing tolerance had nothing to do with my parents, family, or politics. While psychological, cultural, and environmental factors may have influenced where, how much, and how often I drank, they weren't the underlying cause of my addiction. I was an alcoholic because of the process of change my body had undergone. Milam compares using psychology as a reason for alcoholism to treating someone with syphilis with therapy intended to weed out the root loneliness that sent him to a whorehouse. Indeed, if I had been raised by strict Baptists and had not started drinking until I was a middle-aged father of ten children, had I had the same genes, I would have gone through the same process.

As I kept reading, the surprises continued. According to experts, AA is the most effective tool to help alcoholics stay sober, yet Milam calls AA "a colossal paradox." On one hand, the organization has done more than any other to help people understand that alcoholism is a treatable disease. It is also the most effective means of achieving long-term sobriety. Yet it also still claims that alcoholism is an illness caused by psychological or emotional problems, which is the last thing a toxic, newly sober alcoholic should hear. The psychological problems—resentment, depression, immaturity—are the *symptoms* of the disease, not the cause.

Even more striking was Milam's research on how alcoholism affects the brain. Milam claims that alcoholics have a malfunction in the liver that causes acetaldehyde, a toxic by-product of alcohol, to build up. The acetaldehyde gets into the bloodstream and then the brain, where something remarkable happens. They combine with brain amines to form something called isoquinolines. "For alcoholics," writes Milam, "the isoquinolines have one characteristic which makes their other properties pale in significance. They are astonishingly like opiates, and researchers suggest that they may act on the opiate receptors in the brain, thus contributing to the addiction of alcohol." [2]

In fact, the slow physiological brain atrophy of alcoholism is what accounts for the erratic and deteriorative behavior and emotional state of its victim—behavior which is mistakenly cited as the reason for the addiction. Some people assume that drunks are people whose crazed creative genius or existential despair lead them to the bottle and addiction, when the truth is that their angst is the consequence rather than the cause of the addiction. "All of the psychopathology of alcoholism, as alcoholism, is of neurological origin," Milam wrote in one article, "but this fact is disguised because alcoholism is never diagnosed until after character and personality are distorted and normal emotions are neurologically augmented to abnormal levels of chronic anguish, fear, resentment, guilt, and depression. It is these distortions that clinically identify alcoholism, not the original character and personality." [3]

Yet the final, most devastating shock was still left. In *Under the Influence,* Milam also discusses the barriers to recovery—what he calls the "protracted withdrawal syndrome." He talks about how it takes months or even years for all the devastating physical effects of alcoholism to clear, and that these effects can be responsible for the person's emotional distress in early recovery—in short, that many emotional problems alcoholics have in early sobriety are the result of the brain and body trying to readjust to the absence of the addictive drug. According to Milam, alcoholics are in need of nutritional supplements for weeks, years, or even a lifetime to help them heal from the ravages of their disease. Without such aid in recuperation, many stay unstable. "When a patient is chronically malnourished, as many alcoholics are, long-term nutritional therapy is obviously required to restore physical and mental health, and ignoring patients' nutritional needs is simply inadequate treatment." [4]

One of the most prevalent instabilities, writes Milam, is hypoglycemia, an inability to process sugar. Hypoglycemics are the opposite of diabetics—they tend to oversecrete insulin when they eat sugar, and the oversecretion causes their blood sugar, or glucose, level to plummet. The results are dire. According to Milam, "If their erratic blood sugar level is not controlled, alcoholics suffer chronic symptoms of depression, irritability, anguish, fatigue, insomnia, headaches, and mental confusion. Worst of all, low blood sugar causes a craving for substances such as alcohol and sweets which can quickly raise the blood sugar and relieve the symptoms. Sober alcoholics, therefore, must learn to control their sugar intake in order to avoid mood fluctuations, anxiety, and depression, and recurring impulses to drink." [5]

What many hypoglycemics who are unaware of their condition discover is that what alleviates these symptoms is another blast of easily absorbed sugar—such as that found in alcohol—which quickly boosts glucose back to normal levels. Unfortunately, the levels fall again hours later, leaving the victim agitated and depressed all over again. According to Milam, the treatment of hypoglycemia is easy—a high protein, low carbohydrate diet.

As I read Milam's description of hypoglycemia, I felt another jolt of shock and a surge of hope. The depression, panic attacks, and irritability were all my symptoms, and they had vanished when I had recently relapsed. I was also putting away sugary foods like a ten-year-old on Halloween. I had Cokes for breakfast and candy bars for dessert. In AA, this was encouraged. In the organization's book *Living Sober,* one of the prescribed cures for a craving is eating something sweet.

The next day, I tested Milam's hypothesis about hypo-glycemia. I forswore sugar, and by noon my anxiety and depression suddenly, as if by magic, lifted. Then I went to the hospital in Bethesda to take a glucose test. During the test they give you a high-sugar drink, then monitor your progress over five hours.

After the test I immediately ate a large meal to counteract the sugar, then went home to do some research. I began to go through my alcoholism books and found something very interesting. Bill Wilson, AA's co-founder, wanted to change the organization after researching the biology of alcoholism.

Wilson, of course, is primarily remembered as the man who concluded that the only way to abstain was by deflating the ego, which was responsible for the will-to-drink, and by working the Twelve Steps.

The emphasis of AA was, and has always been, on correcting the "character defects" that many recovering alcoholics believed were the root cause of addiction. "We reluctantly come to grips with those serious character flaws that made problem drinkers of us in the first place," Wilson once wrote, "flaws which must be dealt with to prevent a retreat into alcoholism once again."

Yet years after writing these words, Wilson changed his tune, coming to loggerheads with the organization he founded about the biology of alcoholism. After Wilson experimented with LSD in the

1950s, Humphry Osmond and Abram Hoffer, the doctors who con-
ducted the experiments, told Wilson about their research indicating
that massive doses of vitamin B-3—niacin—had produced remarkable results in treating alcoholics by helping to stabilize blood sugar
levels. Wilson already suspected that alcoholism and hypoglycemia
were related, and when he heard of the B-3 experiments "he grew
wildly enthusiastic," according to *'Pass It On.'* Wilson began
extolling B-3 at AA meetings and allegedly claimed that he would be
best remembered not for AA but for his promotion of B-3 therapy.

Unfortunately, AA didn't share Wilson's enthusiasm. The AA
General Service Board claimed that Wilson was in violation of the
Traditions he himself had written, which forbid AA to have an
"opinion on outside issues." At the 1967 AA conference, there was
a recommendation that the organization separate itself from the
B-3 controversy. Wilson grudgingly complied, though he didn't
stop his research. His last paper about niacin was written just
before his death in 1971 and published posthumously.

I was about to call Ronnie, who was an aspiring doctor, and
tell him what I had found, when the phone rang.

"Mr. Judge? This is Dr. Phillips at Suburban Hospital. We just
got your test results back, and I must say that I'm a bit stunned. In
the fifth hour of your test, your glucose level dropped from 81 to
20 milligrams."

"Is that bad?"

"Let me put it this way, your glucose level should always be around one hundred. Anything below sixty is bad, and anything below forty is dangerous. In twenty years of medicine, I've never seen a twenty. You're lucky you're not in a coma."

"My God," I said. "What should I do?"

"There's really nothing you can do, except always make sure you have access to food when you need it. There's really no medicine for it."

"So could hypoglycemia this severe have caused problems that appeared mental—like depression and panic attacks?"

"Without question. Your brain relies on a steady flow of glucose to survive, and when the levels drop that low, it sends out distress signals. If you're having depression and panic attacks, this could be the root of it. In fact, I'd bet on it."

I hung up and immediately called my editor at the *Post*. I knew a great story when I saw one. I explained everything that had happened to me. I didn't care about revealing that I was an alcoholic. Society's every perception about alcoholism was wrong, and I wanted to do a piece on it.

"Wow, that sounds interesting," Sardello said. "But let me get back to you."

"Why do you have to get back to me? Just let me write the thing, then print it."

"I'll call you back."

An hour later, he called. "Look, I'm sorry," he said. "I checked with our science editor, and he just can't defend the story."

I was shocked. "The science editor?" I said. "What are you talking about?"

"I just had a long talk with him about the story you want to do. He says there isn't enough evidence to support your opinion that alcoholism is purely biological."

"Wait a minute," I said, trying to believe what was happening. "Let me see if I have this straight. I want to do a piece for the opinion page of the paper about how I feel that alcoholism is a genetic and biological disease whose onset has nothing to do with psychology. Granted, part of my angle is my own personal experience, but I'm backing it up with the work of Dr. Milam, a man who has been working in the field of alcoholism for twenty years. He has run a hospital and his own recovery program, and he has written a book that's gone through fifteen printings. Jesus Christ, Sardello, you run op-eds by guys like Henry Kissinger that are the worst kind of demagogic tripe and have absolutely no backing in fact, and you don't want to run a piece questioning the status quo of alcoholism treatment and cultural perception that's backed with the research of an expert? Are you shitting me?"

"I don't know what to tell you, Mark. He just doesn't think the piece will stand. He thinks it will be too slanted."

"Listen, you dense son of a bitch, we are talking about an *opinion* piece. It's supposed to be slanted. God almighty, how did you ever get a job at that paper?"

He hung up.

That night, I met Ronnie at a meeting in Georgetown. If the *Post* wouldn't listen, at least AA would. Surely after so many years the organization was ready to see the error of censuring Wilson and was ready to recognize that alcoholism is genetic and biochemical, not the result of character defects.

When the leader asked for volunteers, my hand shot up. I went on about what I had learned about hypoglycemia and the biology of addiction. This was genetic, I said, physiological. There was no need to try to find some emotional or psychological problem that "triggered our alcoholism." We were set up from birth. On top of that, the psychological problems of people in recovery were just the result of the addiction, not its cause.

When I finished talking, there was a deep silence in the room. After a few seconds, a young woman sitting across from me raised her hand.

"Hi, my name's Karen and I'm an alcoholic."

"Hi, Karen."

"At the risk of getting into crosstalk, I feel like I have to say something about what was just said."

Great, I thought. My first fan.

"I think this is a spiritual disease," she said.

Around her, heads started nodding.

"I mean, all that medical stuff is great, but at its heart, alcoholism is about character defects, just like the Big Book says. I do think that in many cases alcoholism is genetic, but not every time. I think there are a lot of alcoholics like me who just drank to the point where they became alcoholics, because they didn't have other ways of coping with their problems."

Now the heads were furiously bobbing up and down. *My God, after my brilliant dissertation, they were actually agreeing with her.*

"I started drinking when I was fourteen," she continued. "I started because my father used to hit us and it was a way to escape."

"Oh Christ, spare me the psychobabble," I barked. "Maybe you were drinking so much because you are alcoholic. Maybe your unique biochemistry caused your high-tolerance drinking, and you're misinterpreting something else as the cause. You're blaming your father."

People were aghast. Interrupting someone, or "crosstalk," was a big no-no in an AA meeting, and verbally abusing someone was unheard of. I didn't care. I was trying to help these people, and they were going to get that help whether they wanted it or not.

Another hand went up, a middle-aged man. "I don't want to turn this into a big debate or a gang up, but I have to agree with

Karen. This is a spiritual disease. And it's not about blaming anyone or anything except ourselves. It was our character defects that
got us drunk, and our character defects and egos that prevented us
from taking responsibility and getting help for many years."

"Bullshit, I said. "This organization refuses to join the twentieth century and realize that alcoholism is genetic and has nothing
to do with character defects or God or anything else. Let me ask
you something, do smokers get addicted because of personal problems? How about heroin addicts? These people get hooked
because of the way the drug reacts in their bodies. Why should
alcohol be different? Maybe some people—namely, alcoholics—
have an addictive reaction to the drug that's not much different
from the way most people react to nicotine or heroin. Maybe—"

"Look," Karen said. "Biology had nothing to do with the
fact that I relapsed four times. That was all me. I chose to take
those drinks rather than get any help."

"But it has *everything* to do with biology. Did you go to
a rehab?"

"No. I detoxed in here."

"No wonder you relapsed. You could be hypoglycemic and
not know it. That could be responsible for your depression and
your relapses."

Just then I felt a strong tap on my shoulder. It was Ronnie.

"Outside," he hissed in my ear.

We got up and went outside. No one cried to see me leave.

"What is it?" I said. "Why did you cut me off?"

"Easy, easy," he said, holding his hands up. "You're taking on too much at once."

He pulled out a cigarette. "Excuse me, but you don't mind if I indulge my genetic, biochemical nicotine habit, do you?"

He lit up, and we sat on the steps.

"So you've been doing a lot of reading," he said. "That's good."

"Apparently not around here, it isn't."

He sat there for a few seconds. "What have you been reading? *Under the Influence?*"

I started. "How did you know?"

"'Cause I've read it, man. It's a good book. It's also very pro-AA."

"Not really. It says AA is a paradox."

"It also says that it's the best thing around for achieving long-term sobriety."

He had me. The book did say that. "Well, I'm not interested in the long-term right now," I said. "I'm worried about all the poor newly sober bastards who are going to come in here and be told they have character defects when they should be in a hospital."

"Look, man, what you have to realize is that AA is not treatment. People come here for recovery, not for treatment."

"That's not true. People *do* come here for treatment. How many times have you heard stories from people who talk about going through detox in AA meetings? Every week. 'I detoxed in the rooms.' It's an AA mantra."

"So you're saying that AA should become a hospital?"

"No. I'm saying that AA should change. It should add a new introduction to the Big Book, written by a doctor who understands the real nature of the illness. And it shouldn't be shy about getting into politics and lobbying. Do you realize how many people we could be helping if we were pushing the facts through? We should be down on Capitol Hill clamoring for legislation, and all over the media. Don't you get it? Our entire concept of addictive illness has changed, and AA hasn't. It's worse than those cowards at the *Post*. Do you have any idea how much good AA could be doing right now? How much it could be changing public perception about alcoholism?"

"I think it's done that already."

"How? By telling the world that all of our problems are spiritually based? Sorry, but that doesn't cut it. We have to drop this ridiculous position that addiction is somehow chemical and spiritual. It can't be both."

"Why not?"

"Because it can't. Either something is biological or it's spiritual. It can't be both."

"Why?"

"It just can't."

"Look man, you're saying that we should be a rehab," he said. "But we're not supposed to be a rehab."

"But don't you see? It's a rehab by default. The culture tells us that when you have a drinking problem you go to AA. It's almost become second nature. The role of rehab has been foisted upon AA whether it likes it or not."

"But if we started acting like a clearinghouse for medical information, it would drive the spirituality right out of AA—the spirituality that most people see as the reason AA works."

"But it *doesn't* work," I shouted. "According to everything I've read, the best estimates for AA have its success rate at 25 percent. That's nothing to brag about."

Ronnie shrugged. "I can't tell you what to do," he said. "I can only tell you what works for me. And I can also tell you that Milam would probably disagree with you."

"Well, I can't do this anymore," I said.

He looked at me sharply. "You're not dropping out?"

"Afraid so."

I stormed off. It was Saturday night and the streets of

Georgetown were crowded with shoppers and bar hoppers. I walked around aimlessly, my eyes focused on the ground. I was feeling so frustrated I wanted to punch something. The answers were in plain sight, yet no one wanted them. Not those idiots at the *Post,* not AA.

I turned a corner and found myself in front of a familiar spot: O'Rourke's.

I decided to go in, just for old-time's sake. It was only nine o'clock, so the place was only about half full. On the weekends, most drinkers didn't begin to come in until after ten.

I sat at the bar. The bartender, a young woman, came over.

"Draft beer," I said.

I couldn't believe I was actually going to do it. After the blackouts, the panic attacks, the admission of alcoholism, the hypoglycemia, I was going to take a drink and do it all over again. I completely understood my illness and knew if I drank I would have panic attacks and probably even black out. Yet I still wanted that comfort zone the drug provided. Although my body had deteriorated to the point where my tolerance was starting to evaporate, I knew that for ten or twenty minutes before blacking out, I could escape. And that was all I wanted.

Still, something prevented me from picking up the glass. I remembered my visit to Dr. Ryan and Milam's description of withdrawal, how the imbalances of early sobriety could make one emotionally volatile. I was able to step back from myself and real-ize that my wild mood swings could be biochemical.

I calmed down a little. Then, out of nowhere, I recalled something I had read in the Big Book that first night I realized I was an alcoholic: A drink would mean insanity or death.

Insanity or death, I thought. Insanity or death.

I wrapped my hands around the cool pint glass. It felt tight and secure, like it belonged there.

I raised the glass to my mouth, then put it down. The bar-tender looked at me sideways from the other end of the bar.

"Help me, God," I whispered under my breath.

"You all right?" the bartender asked.

I looked at her. "No," I said quietly. "I'm not."

"What's the problem?"

"I can't drink this."

She looked at the pint. "What's wrong with it?"

"Nothing," I stammered. "I just can't drink it.

Just then, I felt a hand on my shoulder.

It was Ronnie. "You know," he said, "after your grand exit I followed you down here. I stood outside for about five minutes wondering what to do. I didn't want to interfere, because your recovery has to be your own. But then I thought about what you were saying, about alcoholism being biological and all that, and that the chemistry of it affects recovery. And I figured that right now, so early in sobriety, you may not know how to deal with things, and a lot of it may be because there's all kinds of toxic junk in your system. But even more importantly, I know what a jerk you are after a bender, and I don't want to have to deal with you when you come crawling back to AA."

"It's hard to believe," I said. "People in AA are still talking about addictive personalities when there is no such thing."

"Well," he said, "I don't want to be one to judge or anything, but it sounds to me like your problem right now is not whether there are addictive personalities or not. It seems to me that your problem is how you're not going to have that drink in the next five minutes."

I looked at the beer.

"Listen," he said, "have you ever thought that diseases, even though biologically based, can have a spiritual component in how they affect the victim? That something like cancer or AIDS—or alcoholism—can change people, causing a spiritual experience that brings them closer to God? And that by doing so these horrible diseases cause them to acknowledge that they had never been spiritual before. Their whole attitude and worldview changed because of a painful *biological* disease. Have you ever thought that it can be both?"

I didn't say anything.

"Look, the trick with AA is to take what you like, leave the rest. It says right there in the Third Tradition—'the only require-ment for A.A. membership is a desire to stop drinking.' That's it. You can think that everything else here is total bullshit. But if you have a desire to stop drinking, you belong here. And it seems to me that right now you have a desire to not drink."

"But people should know," I said. "The entire culture has to be reeducated."

"Then reeducate them," he said. "If you think it will help drunks, go ahead. Maybe if I ever get back to med school and get through, we can be a team. But you can do it without being so self-ish. You know, even if you think your character defects didn't cause your alcoholism, you still have them as a result of your drinking—not to mention the flaws you had before drinking that stunted your emotional growth. Everyone has flaws, but you need to work on yours to stay sober. And the only way you're going to stay sober, the only way to recover from this disease, is with the support and guid-ance of your friends, family, a higher power, and people who understand the permanent threat of addiction. Like the people in AA. We alcoholics need each other. You claim to have all this pro-found knowledge about alcoholism, and all you want to use it for is causing fights at AA meetings and getting your name in the paper. Why don't you use it to help people?"

"Because people don't want to listen."

"Oh, I don't know about that. They might not want to be

preached at—I don't think anyone does. But there's a way of conveying your information without alienating people. You might actually help a few souls. Jesus, man, this is all new to you. Give it time to sink in. You're not going to change the world tonight."

Just then, the front door opened.

It was Shane. He saw me and came over. "Why aren't I surprised that you're the first one here?" he said.

"What are you talking about?"

"It's the 10th. The Prep reunion, remember?"

The Prep reunion. I had completely forgotten.

"I even brought the yearbook," he said. He handed me the large blue book from our senior year at Prep. I looked at the pictures of us at the beach and at basketball games, laughing and dancing at parties.

"Man," Shane said, peering over my shoulder. "Those were the days."

Indeed, they were. We had been fearless and crazy, staying up all night laughing and drinking like there was no tomorrow. It had been a magical time, and now it was over for me.

Or at least the drinking part of it was over. I flipped through the book until I came to my own picture. Below it I had put a quote from *The Lord of the Rings*.

Suddenly, I felt a surge of hope. I recalled that at the end of *The Lord of the Rings*, Frodo the hobbit does destroy the evil ring that had been destroying him. But ultimately he only did so against his will, and the experience left him changed. He did not return home the same creature he had been when he left. He had been wounded and would never regain the innocence he once had. A part of him had died, but even as it had, he had been born into a new and different kind of life—a wider, more humble and spiritual life.

Ronnie called the bartender over and ordered two sodas. Then he pulled a tape out of his pocket and asked her to play the first song. She put the tape in the deck above the bar, and the room was suddenly filled with the seductive chug of swing.

"One O'clock Jump," Ronnie said, tapping his foot.

The bartender made a funny face. "What is this stuff?" she asked.

"It's swing, man," Ronnie said. "And you can dance to it. Come out here—my friend Mr. Judge here, a debonair gentleman, will show you how."

"Oh no," I muttered.

"Come on," Ronnie said. "Show her your stuff."

Shane looked at Ronnie. "Are you telling me this guy knows how to dance?"

"Show 'em," Ronnie said.

"Oh, what the hell," I said. I led the bartender out from behind the bar. Although she didn't know what to do, I felt sure that I could teach her, the way Ruth had taught me.

"Okay, just follow me," I said.

We started to dance, moving around the dry wood floor.

"You're swingin', man!" Ronnie shouted.

"I don't believe it," Shane muttered.

"Believe it, man," Ronnie said. "The boy was born to dance."

By now people at the bar were clapping in time. I threw my head back and laughed out loud. It was like hearing music for the first time.

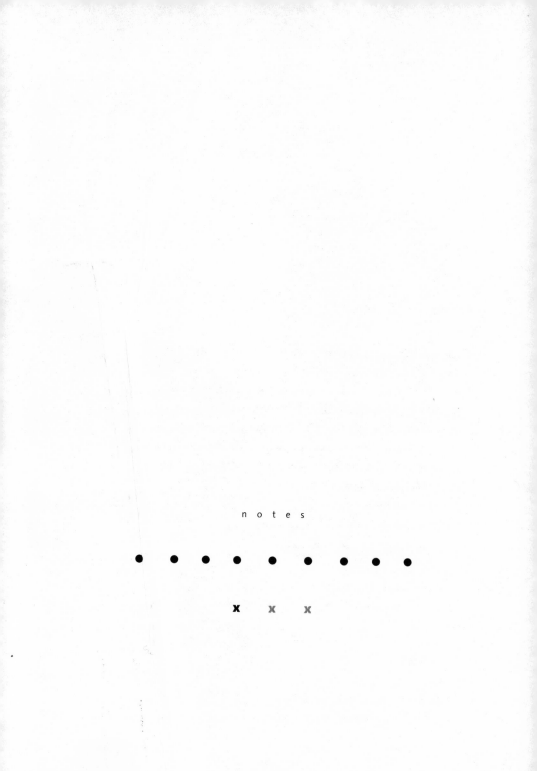

notes

chapter eight
Giving Up the Sauce

1. Ernest Kurtz, *Not-God: A History of Alcoholics Anonymous* (Center City, Minn.: Hazelden, 1979), 19–20. First published in William Griffith Wilson et al., *Alcoholics Anonymous Comes of Age* (New York: Alcoholics Anonymous World Services, Inc., 1957), 63.

2. *'Pass It On,' The Story of Bill Wilson and How the A.A. Message Reached the World* (New York: Alcoholics Anonymous World Services, Inc., 1980), 370.

3. *'Pass It On,'* 375.

4. Tom Dardis, *The Thirsty Muse: Alcohol and the American Writer* (New York: Ticknor and Fields, 1989), 7.

chapter nine
Choose Life

1. James R. Milam and Katherine Ketcham, *Under the Influence: A Guide to the Myths and Realities of Alcoholism* (Seattle: Madrona Publishers, 1981), 51–52.

2. Joan Mathews Larson, *Seven Weeks to Sobriety* (New York: Ballantine Books, 1992), 13.

3. Milam and Ketcham, *Under the Influence,* 34.

4. James R. Milam, "The Alcoholism Revolution," *Professional Counselor Magazine,* October 1992.

5. Milam and Ketcham, *Under the Influence,* 139

6. Milam and Ketcham, *Under the Influence,* 140.

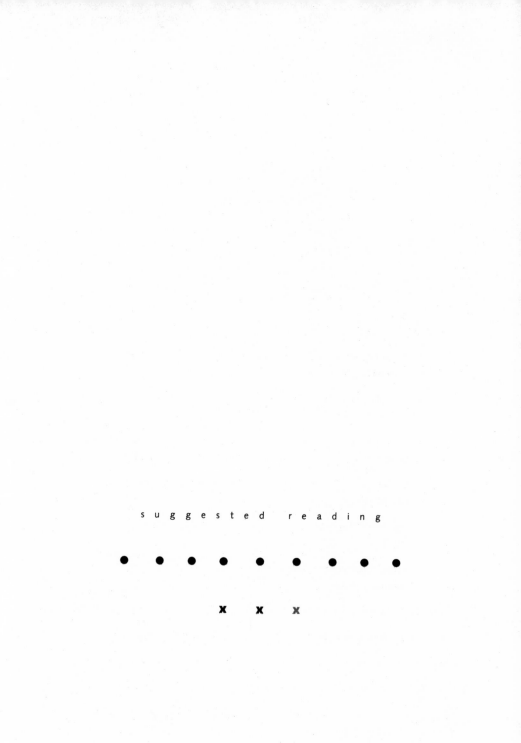

suggested reading

Alcoholics Anonymous World Services, Inc. *Alcoholics Anonymous.* 3rd ed. New York: Alcoholics Anonymous World Services, Inc., 1976.

———. *Twelve Steps and Twelve Traditions.* 3rd ed. New York: Alcoholics Anonymous World Services, Inc. 1981.

———. *'Pass It On,' The Story of Bill Wilson and How the A.A. Message Reached the World.* New York: Alcoholics Anonymous World Services, Inc., 1984.

Dardis, Tom. *The Thirsty Muse: Alcohol and the American Writer.* New York: Ticknor & Fields, 1989.

Kurtz, Ernest. *Not–God: A History of Alcoholics Anonymous.* Center City, Minn.: Hazelden, 1979.

Kurtz, Ernest, and Katherine Ketcham. *The Spirituality of Imperfection.* New York: Bantam, 1992.

Larson, Joan Mathews. *Seven Weeks to Sobriety.* New York: Ballantine Books, 1992.

London, Jack. *John Barleycorn, or Alcoholic Memoirs.* New York: Penguin, 1990.

Mazor, Julian. *Washington and Baltimore.* New York: Alfred A. Knopf, 1968.

Menchen, H. L. *The American Scene: A Reader.* New York: Vintage Books, 1982.

Milam, James R., and Katherine Ketcham. *Under the Influence: A Guide to the Myths and Realities of Alcoholism.* New York: Bantam Books, 1983.

Thompson, Hunter S. *The Great Shark Hunt.* New York: Warner Books, 1986.

Tolkien, J. R. R. *The Lord of the Rings.* New York: Ballantine, 1965.

about the author

x   x   x

Mark Gauvreau Judge

Mark Gauvreau Judge is an award-winning journalist whose work has appeared in the Washington *Post,* the *Weekly Standard, Sojourners,* and other publications. He lives in the Washington, DC, area.